The Wild Horses
of Corolla

THE HOOFPRINTS GUIDE TO

The Wild Horses *of* Corolla

Written and Illustrated by
Bonnie U. Gruenberg

The Hoofprints Guide to the Wild Horses of Chincoteague

Copyright © 2015 by Bonnie U. Gruenberg.

ISBN 13: 978-1-941700-14-3

Library of Congress Control Number: 2015949490

Published by Quagga Press, an imprint of Synclitic Media, LLC
1646 White Oak Road • Strasburg, PA 17579 • www.quaggapress.com

Also by the author
  The Wild Horse Dilemma: Conflicts and Controversies of the Atlantic Coast Herds (Quagga Press, 2015)
  The Hoofprints Guide Series (Quagga Press, 2015)
    Assateague • Chincoteague • Corolla
    Ocracoke • Shackleford Banks • Cumberland Island
  Essentials of Prehospital Maternity Care (Prentice Hall, 2005)
  Birth Emergency Skills Training: Manual for Out-of-hospital Providers (Birth Guru/Birth Muse, 2008)
  Hoofprints in the Sand Wild Horses of the Atlantic Coast (as Bonnie S. Urquhart; Eclipse Press, 2002)
  The Midwife's Journal (Birth Guru/Birth Muse, 2009)
  Hoofprints in the Sand: Wild Horses of the Atlantic Coast, Kindle Edition (Quagga Press, 2014)
  Wild Horses of the Atlantic Coast: An Intimate Portrait, Kindle Edition (Quagga Press, 2014)

Forthcoming
  Wild Horse Vacations: Your Guide to the Atlantic Wild Horse Trail with Local Attractions and Amenities(Quagga Press, 2015)
    Vol. 1: Assateague, MD | Chincoteague, VA | Corolla, NC
    Vol. 2: Ocracoke, NC | Shackleford Banks, NC | Cumberland Island, GA
  Wild Horses! A Kids' Guide to the East Coast Herds (Quagga Press, 2015)
  Birth Emergency Skills Training, 2nd Edition (Synclitic Press, 2015).

Introduction

"There are a lot of cottonmouth water moccasins in this area, so keep your eyes down and watch where you step," said Wesley.

The thigh-high water in the flooded meadow tugged gently at my fishing waders as the wild horse manager guided me to an otherwise inaccessible section of the equine sanctuary. Off in the distance, we could see the contours of grazing horses . . . four, five, and over there— a sixth. Suddenly there was a movement, and what had first appeared to be a dusky shadow beneath a black mare unfolded itself into a newborn foal, no more than a day old.

I broke into a delighted grin, but Wesley frowned. "That mare had two other colts, and both died as newborns. I wonder if they were unable to nurse." We approached the pair in a sweeping arc, trying to assess the foal's health without alarming the mare. She was not at all pleased with our proximity to her gangly-limbed youngster and swiftly ushered him to a more secluded spot. There, she extended her hind leg in an invitation to nurse and nudged her small son into position. When he found the teat, he suckled vigorously. He was off to a good start. In the months to come, it became clear that this colt would survive and perhaps add his genes to the unbroken lineage flowing from ancestral Colonial Spanish Horses through its wild descendants.

When I first started researching the wild horses in the mid-1990s, I was surprised to find that wild horses lived on a number of Atlantic barrier islands and had once ranged along much of the Atlantic coast. They made their first hoofprints there not long after the arrival of early European settlers, and in time they ran free on innumerable North American islands and peninsulas from the Caribbean to Canada. I learned that small herds remained on the coast of Virginia, North Carolina, Maryland, and Georgia; on Sable Island, off Nova Scotia, Canada; and on Great Abaco Island in the Bahamas. Each population of horses has its own character, its own history, and its own set of problems. In most cases, these animals have made a unique contribution to local history, and each herd has its own detractors and defenders.

After my first book, *Hoofprints in the Sand: Wild Horses of the Atlantic Coast*, was published in 2002 by Eclipse Press, I dove in deeper, interviewing experts, evaluating the evidence, and monitoring the herds. I explored management conflicts that encompass political, economic, and cultural issues as well as purely scientific ones. I studied storms and shipwrecks, equine behavior and genetics, history, epidemiology, barrier-island dynamics, sea-level rise, beach development, and the perpetual clash of viewpoints. I pored over hundreds of documents, from historical papers to scholarly articles to court transcripts, so that I might accurately present the pertinent issues. Distilling all this information, I tried to present all sides of the issues fairly so that readers might reach their own conclusions. The result is *The Wild Horse Dilemma: Conflicts and Controversies of the Atlantic Coast Herds* (Quagga Press, 2015) the most comprehensive work ever published about these horses.

Wild Horse Dilemma is exhaustively researched, copiously documented, and peer-reviewed; but at 600 pages, it may be too long for many people eager to learn about a particular herd. For readers with limited time, I created the Hoofprints Series. Excerpted from *Wild Horse Dilemma* and containing additional photographs, each Hoofprints book presents a single Atlantic Coast herd in sufficient detail to satisfy both the layman and the academic.

I take all my wild-horse photographs though telephoto lenses that let me keep my distance. When horses approach, I retreat. My goal has been to remain so peripheral to their lives, they will forget that I am nearby. Because countless people have stroked them, fed them, and lured them, some can be momentarily docile, occasionally indifferent, or routinely bold and pushy in the presence of people. As anyone bitten or trampled can attest, they are no less wild than horses that avoid human contact. When we impose ourselves and our desires on their lives, when we habituate them to our presence, when we teach them to come to us for food and attention, we rob them of their wildness. When we treat them as we would their domestic counterparts, we miss the opportunity to observe them in a natural state, that is, to appreciate the things that make them irresistibly attractive. We miss the very point of driving past thousands of their tame kin to seek them out. We create something like a petting zoo hazardous to us and to them. If we truly love and respect wild creatures, we must learn to stand back and enjoy watching them from afar. Only then can they—and we—know the real meaning of wildness.

As the earth's dominant species, we have the power to preserve or destroy the wildlife of the world and the ecosystems in which they live. The choices we make regarding wild horses are far-reaching. We alter their destiny whether we act or choose to do nothing. We can begin to deal wisely with wild horses by understanding the facts and discovering how the threads of their existence are woven into the tapestry of life. Only through understanding can we hope to make rational, educated decisions about the welfare of these fascinating, inspiring animals.

Bonnie U. Gruenberg
Strasburg, Pennsylvania
September 12, 2015

Corolla

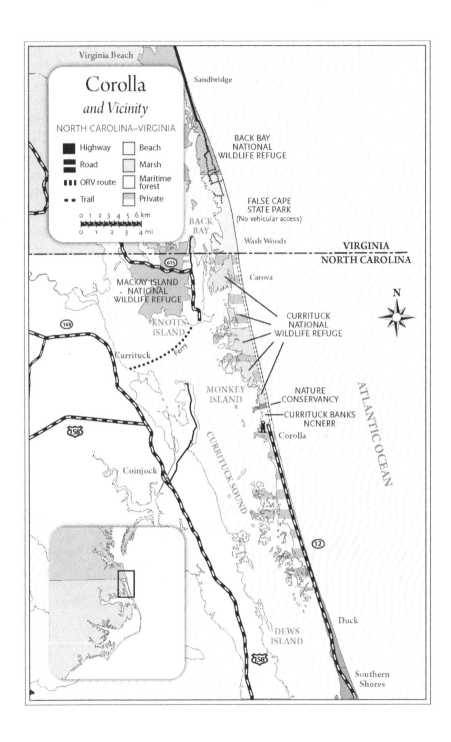

Corolla
and Vicinity

NORTH CAROLINA–VIRGINIA

Highway   Beach
Road   Marsh
ORV route Maritime forest
Trail   Private

0 1 2 3 4 5 6 km
0 1 2 3 4 mi

Virginia Beach
Sandbridge
BACK BAY NATIONAL WILDLIFE REFUGE
FALSE CAPE STATE PARK (No vehicular access)
BACK BAY
Wash Woods

VIRGINIA
NORTH CAROLINA

MACKAY ISLAND NATIONAL WILDLIFE REFUGE
Carova
KNOTTS ISLAND
CURRITUCK NATIONAL WILDLIFE REFUGE

168

Currituck
Ferry

MONKEY ISLAND
NATURE CONSERVANCY
CURRITUCK BANKS NCNERR
Corolla

158

Coinjock

CURRITUCK SOUND

ATLANTIC OCEAN

12

DEWS ISLAND

158

Duck

Southern Shores

Around the time Paul Revere made his famous ride in Massachusetts on a Narragansett Pacer, a girl on a Banker Pony is said to have made a similar trek to become a heroine of the Revolutionary War. The legend, passed along through oral traditions, tells of a teenager named Betsy Dowdy who rode her mare from Currituck Banks to Hertford, North Carolina, on a cold winter night to inform the militia of the threat from British troops.

In the winter of 1775, John Murray, 4th Earl of Dunmore and royal governor of Virginia, had fled his palace in Williamsburg and begun making hostile raids on southeastern Virginia. He planned to best Colonel William Woodford of the 2nd Virginia Regiment at Great Bridge, then attack the Albemarle Sound region of North Carolina to obtain supplies and mounts for his soldiers. Locals were distraught, fearing that if Dunmore's campaign succeeded he would leave them destitute between harvests. Only the Perquimans Militia of General William Skinner had the power to help repel the attack, and it was too far away to respond in time.

The legend says that Betsy Dowdy, an Outer Banks teenager living opposite Knotts Island, heard of Dunmore's plans and resolved to gallop her rugged Banker mare, Black Bess, bareback through the night to alert the troops.

Creecy (1901, p. 6) tells her story:

> Down the beach she went, Black Bess doing her accustomed work. She reached the point opposite Church's Island, dashed into the shallow ford of Currituck Sound, and reached the shore of the Island . . . Through the divide, on through Camden, the twinkling stars her only light, over Lamb's old ferry, into Pasquotank, by the "narrows" (now Elizabeth City) to Hartsford's ford, up the Highlands of Perquimans, onto Yoepim creek, and General William Skinner's hospitable home was reached.

Betsy is said to have ridden 51 mi/82 km bareback through the dark winter night to Gen. Skinner's headquarters. Skinner dispatched his troops to meet Lord Dunmore's army, and they won the battle of

Great Bridge. There is no documentation to verify the story, but the legend is a treasured part of Carolina coastal folklore.

In 2012, the author gained insight into what Betsy might have experienced. Riding with Steve Edwards of Mill Swamp Indian Horses in Smithfield, Va., who breeds domesticated Banker horses, she galloped a once-wild Corolla stallion named Manteo through a moonless Virginia wood in darkness so deep she literally could not see her hand in front of her face. He ran effortlessly along a pitch-dark forest trail over exposed roots and rocks, through deep mud and into pools of standing water up to his hocks. The little stallion, an athlete accustomed to 50-mi/80-km trail riding events, moved tirelessly at speed for the better part of an hour, never faltering, never distracted or disobedient. Effectively blinded by the night, she had no choice but to trust a wild-born Banker stallion that could see the way while she could not. It was a profound experience that she will remember always.

Free-roaming horses have inhabited the North Carolina Outer Banks for centuries. At one time, they numbered in the thousands, ranging over the 175-mile/282-km span of islands from Shackleford Banks north beyond False Cape in Virginia. As recently as 1926, a writer for *National Geographic* stated that 5,000–6,000 horses roamed the Outer Banks. They grazed primarily in the marshes, drifting out to the beach in the summer months to escape biting insects and catch the sea breeze. Like their human neighbors, these horses were rugged, tenacious, and independent. Until the 20th century, horses, cattle, hogs, sheep, and goats far outnumbered humans on this difficult-to-homestead barrier island chain. Once or twice a year, locals held roundups for branding to establish ownership of new calves and foals. The rest of the time, the animals were unattended.

On Currituck Banks, the northernmost reach of the Outer Banks, the surviving horses are strikingly Spanish in appearance—short-backed, deep-chested, and wide between the eyes—in shades of black, brown, bay, sorrel or chestnut. They are long-strided and very intelligent. There is no question that Banker Horses carry the blood of Spanish breeds brought to the New World in the 15th and 16th centuries, but how foundation stock reached the Banks is a topic of hot dispute. Some people believe that the first horses were left behind

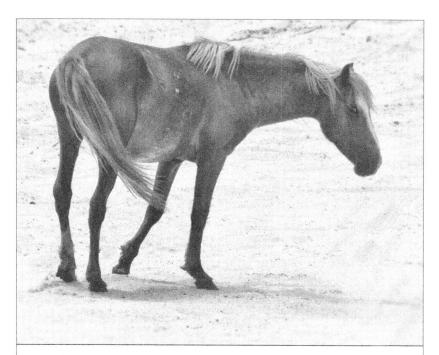

The wild Colonial Spanish Horses of Currituck Banks are a very old strain of a very rare American breed.

by the first explorers or swam ashore from early shipwrecks. Others assert that horses arrived with later colonists who placed them on the barrier islands to graze.

Throughout the 1500s, European explorers of several nationalities sailed the waters north of Cape Romain, South Carolina, including Chesapeake Bay, searching for places to establish a colony or for a passage linking the Atlantic with the Pacific. These scouting ships probably carried few, if any, horses. Although Spain mostly confined its colonizing efforts in the eastern United States to Florida, Georgia, and South Carolina, it did send expeditions farther north. The Eastern Seaboard, however, seemed relatively valueless to Spanish authorities because it offered little gold, no large cities to loot, and no concentrated populations to enslave.

Some speculate that Spaniards attempted to colonize the coast of North Carolina and left horses behind when the colonies failed. Most historians believe this is unlikely. In 1526 Lucas Vázquez de Ayllón established two short-lived settlements. The first may have been as far north as the mouth of the Cape Fear River, and the second was probably in South Carolina; but both are a long way from the Outer Banks. Spanish Jesuits from Florida established a mission on the lower Chesapeake Bay in 1570, but Indians killed all nine priests the next year. None of these brief settlements is a likely source for the Banker Horses.

Aside from Verrazzano's account of a short visit in 1524, the historical record offers few pre-settlement descriptions of the Outer Banks. On New Year's Day (March 25), 1584, Queen Elizabeth I granted Sir Walter Raleigh a huge tract of North America from South Carolina to Nova Scotia, territory claimed by Spain. Unwilling to undertake blindly the risks of colonization, which ranged from expensive failure to war with the most powerful country in Europe, Raleigh dispatched a reconnaissance mission. Two ships under Philip Amadas and Arthur Barlowe set sail on April 27 to explore the coast, evaluate potential settlement sites, and bring back news that might attract support. Barlowe's 1584 account is vague and contains obvious anachronisms, e.g., *Virginia*, a name not applied to the area till 1585, and it seems to include snippets of Verrazzano's 60-year-old narrative. These insertions suggest either that Barlowe wrote his account well after the mission had ended or that he, Raleigh, or someone else embellished it for publication.

There is no mention of livestock pre-dating colonization in any document from the period. Barlowe, in describing the bounty that he found on the Outer banks in 1584, wrote that it "had many goodly woods, full of Deere, Conies, Hares, and Fowle, euen in the middest of Summer, in incredible aboundance" (Quinn, 1955, p. 96). Francis L. Hawks misquoted this passage in his seminal *History of North Carolina* (1857), putting "horses" in one of two places (pp. 82, 88) where Barlowe had written "hares." This transcription error has been perpetuated by subsequent writers who cite it as evidence that horses were living on the Banks when English colonists arrived.

Barlowe was pressed to describe the New World in optimistic terms so that Raleigh might secure backing for colonization, and to justify the time the party had spent exploring a small fraction of Raleigh's grant. He extolled the abundant grapes, waterfowl, and timber and described the native people in great detail. One imagines that if horses had been present, Barlowe would have provided an enthusiastic description.

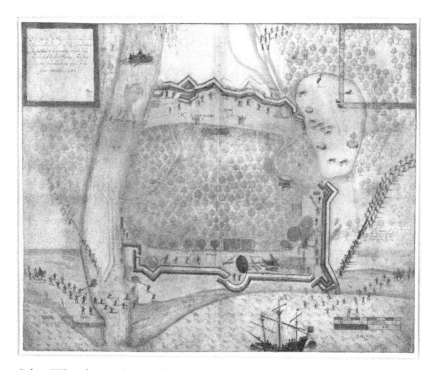

John White's graphite, ink, and watercolor depiction of the fortified camp at Tallaboa Bay, Puerto Rico (1585), shows horses that the Grenville expedition had taken from Spanish colonists. At bottom right, the flagship *Tiger* is anchored. In the bottom left corner, Grenville ("The General"), mounted on a stolen Spanish horse, returns with a party of foot soldiers. Courtesy of the Trustees of the British Museum.

Records of early expeditions are seldom straightforward. The main source of information about the 1585 Grenville expedition is a spotty narrative of unknown authorship. The expedition left England on April 9. From May 12 to 23 or 24, the Englishmen laid over in temporary fortifications at Tallaboa Bay, Puerto Rico, which John White immortalized with a watercolor illustration depicting horses in a corral, among other things. The entry for May 22 describes a tense meeting with local Spaniards, during which Grenville "dispatched 20 footemen towards them, and two horsemen of ours, mounted vpon Spanish horses, which wee before had taken . . . on the Iland" (Quinn, 1955, p. 182). White's painting does not show, and the narrative does not mention, other livestock during the stay on Puerto Rico. Grenville tried to trade with the locals, perhaps for additional livestock; when they refused, he started a forest fire.

En route to Hispaniola to complete his provisioning, Grenville stopped to seize two Spanish ships, ransom his captives, and dig salt. In early June, he arrived at Isabela (in what is now the Dominican Republic) and traded for "horses [stallions], mares, kine [cows], buls, goates, swine, sheepe, bul hides, sugar, ginger, pearle, tabacco, and such like commodities of the Iland" (Quinn, 1955, p. 187). Spanish accounts add mules, calves, and dogs to the list.

Grenville left 107 men on Roanoke Island, the first English colony in North America. Under Governor Ralph Lane, the colonists explored, inventoried natural resources, and antagonized Native Americans. By late spring, 1586, they had probably devoured any remaining livestock, and they were starving. Lane sent half his men to the Banks to find sustenance in the sea. On a disastrous search for gold in the interior, Lane and his party ate their guard dogs, sassafras leaves, and ultimately nothing.

When Sir Francis Drake offered them passage to England a few weeks later, they accepted in such haste that they left three men behind, and impatient sailors threw the colonists' irreplaceable maps and papers overboard. In one stroke, Drake destroyed the Lane colony by removing it two weeks before relief arrived and destroyed most of the information the colonists had gathered in nearly a year of exploration. Further, his plundering tour of Spanish holdings to the south set into motion a series of events that ultimately prevented timely resupply of the 1587 colony. As in Ayllón's case, we can reasonably conclude that desperate settlers, natives, or the elements consumed any horses that had survived the trip before they could establish a self-sustaining herd.

In April 1587 John White sailed west again, this time as governor of a colony, including families and children, to be founded on Chesapeake Bay. He stopped at Roanoke Island in late July to confer with 15 men that Grenville had stationed to guard Lane's abandoned settlement. The men, however had apparently succumbed or fled; he found only bones and dilapidated buildings. Worse, his pilot unexpectedly refused to take the colonists farther, forcing White to establish his colony on Roanoke. Soon after the birth of his granddaughter Virginia Dare, the first English child native to the New World, White returned to England to obtain supplies and recruit new settlers.

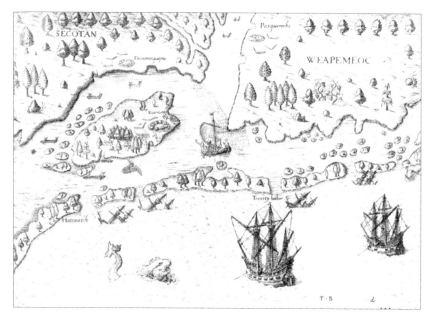

Theodor De Bry (1590) brought John White's paintings to the European public by converting them to reproducible engravings. De Bry never beheld the New World, but he apparently felt free to embellish White's faithful depictions. "The arriual of the Englishemen in Virginia," above, has no known surviving original and bears no clear connection to any of the Raleigh voyages. The tree symbols with which De Bry covered the Outer Banks do not appear on White's maps and may be as true to life as the sea monster at lower left.

Privateer William Irish led another expedition that apparently preceded White's. Alonso Ruiz, a seaman on a vessel that Irish had captured off Cuba in June 1587, later recounted a three-day stop in Virginia during which his captors "found traces of cattle and a stray dark-brown mule" (Quinn, 1955, p. 782). The location of this layover remains unclear. Unaware of White's diversion, Irish may have gone straight to Chesapeake Bay and discovered relics of the old Spanish mission, abandoned 15 years earlier. If Irish likewise took a detour to Roanoke Island and arrived before White, he would have found no settlers, but might have seen livestock. If he arrived after White, he would have seen White's ships, which were anchored offshore until August 28. A Spanish party from St. Augustine visited the Outer Banks in 1588 after searching Chesapeake Bay for the rumored English incursion, but it reported no settlers or livestock in either place.

Thomas Harriot, the Lane colony's chief scientist, seems to say in his *Briefe and True Report*, probably written in 1587, that one English colony had provisions for a year, and comparable rations should sustain successors for a similar interval:

> If that those which shall thit[h]er trauaile to inhabite and plant bee but reasonably prouided for the first yere as those that are which were transported the last, and beeing these doe vse but that diligence and care as is requisite, and as they may with eese: There is no doubt but for the time following they may haue victuals that is excellent good and plentie enough, some more Englishe sortes of cattaile also hereafter, as some have bene before, and are there yet remaining, may and shall bee God willing thit[h]er transported. . . . (1590, p. 32)

Because contemporary writers often referred to all livestock as cattle, it is unclear whether "Englishe sortes of cattaile" denoted bovids or other animals. It is also unclear which colonies Harriot meant, for no Roanoke colony seems to have been "reasonably prouided." The 1585 settlers fled after 11 months of hardship, and the 1587 colonists were so desperate for provisions that they sent Governor White himself back to England "for the better and sooner obtaining of supplies, and other necessaries" (Quinn, 1955, p. 533).

Does Harriot's report indicate that colonists in the 1580s brought animals with them from England? If so, it is unique. Did Ruiz's account indicate that livestock outlasted the 1585 colonists? Clearly, through the 1580s domestic animals were in short supply, and starvation threatened at every turn. Grenville incurred risk and expense acquiring livestock in a hostile region in 1585, and White was unsuccessful in his efforts to obtain more in 1587. Their efforts would have been pointless if they already had English livestock on board. Further, the introduction of English livestock by Roanoke colonists would not explain the presence of predominantly Spanish horses on the Outer Banks in later centuries.

Handicapped by lack of funds and delayed by the attack of the Spanish Armada, White finally returned in 1590, without supplies or settlers, to find the site abandoned. He reported no signs of livestock. It appears unlikely that domestic animals remained on the Outer Banks after 1590. The fate of the Lost Colony is still a mystery.

Historically, Banker horses were generally short in stature and extremely rugged, like their Spanish ancestors. Drawing by the author.

Stick writes that when White sailed from the Banks, the English left the area "in the undisputed possession of the native Indians for another seventy-five years" (1958, p. 21). But by defeating the Spanish Armada in 1588, England cleared the way to colonize North America. Jamestown, founded in 1607, was the first of a new wave of English settlements along the coast. Some failed, but most succeeded.

The North Carolina coast has been inhabited for at least 10,000 years. At the time of European contact, the East Coast was home to diverse tribes representing three different linguistic families. The native people encountered at Roanoke Island and later at Jamestown and Plymouth spoke Algonquian languages. Iroquoian-speaking tribes such as the Tuscarora lived to the west. Natives to the south spoke Siouan. Neighboring languages could be as different as English and Arabic, and linguistic barriers fostered hostility.

These native groups fought viciously against one another and among themselves. Barlowe, probably no stranger to combat, was surprised by the ferocity of their battles. Wars among the indigenous people, he noted, were "very cruell, and bloodie, by reason whereof, and of their ciuill dissentions, which haue happened of late yeeres amongest them, the people are maruelously wasted, and in some places, the Countrey left desolate" (Quinn, 1955, p. 113). The situation had not improved more than a century later, when John Lawson (1709, p. 225) linked the natives' continual hostility to communication problems:

> [T]he continual Wars these Savages maintain, one Nation against another, which sometimes hold for some Ages, killing and making Captives, till they become so weak thereby, that they are forced to make Peace for want of Recruits . . . and the Difference of Languages, that is found amongst these Heathens, seems altogether strange. For it often appears, that every dozen Miles, you meet with an Indian Town, that is quite different from the others you last parted withal. . . .

Fragmentation weakened the indigenous peoples and rendered them vulnerable to displacement and extermination by Old World invaders.

Upon encountering native cultures, Europeans, like any people, fit what they observed into their own intellectual and cultural framework. Consequently, much of what we know about these tribes is based on misconceptions and assumptions. Native languages often perplexed the European ear, and colonists often confused the names of people, places, and fragments of conversation. For example, the English believed that the name of the territory they were exploring was *Wingandacon* until Harriot learned more Carolina Algonquian and concluded that the term meant "You wear fancy clothes." Later scholars suggested that it really related to evergreens. Likewise, John White's paintings offer honest portrayals of extinct cultures and vanished landscapes. But some of White's work survives only in engravings by Theodor De Bry, who lived in England only briefly and never crossed the Atlantic. What we see is filtered through White's and De Bry's perceptions and our own.

Seventeenth-century settlers on the Eastern Seaboard came by long, difficult routes across the Atlantic, usually without livestock, and often purchased farm animals from Spanish ranches in the Caribbean. The cattle, hogs, sheep, goats, and horses raised there were of high quality, bred for hardiness, and much more likely to survive the shorter voyage to the colonies than animals shipped directly from Europe. As in Virginia, North Carolina colonists allowed their livestock to run free; and as in Virginia, roaming livestock soon became a nuisance, not only to other colonists, but also to the native people.

Lee wrote (2008, p. 48), "free ranging stock fostered local tensions. The lands into which colonists advanced were invariably occupied, and foraging cattle and hogs refused to abide by the spatial boundaries that humans created."

Virtually all authorities on Outer Banks history agree that early settlers, mostly small farmers in search of land, migrated down from the Chesapeake area in search of land on which to graze livestock. In July, 1653, Roger Green led a group from Virginia to establish a settlement in what is now North Carolina, alongside the Quakers and other refugees that had left Virginia to escape persecution of those who did not follow the Church of England. These refugees and colonists probably took horses with them. By the mid-1600s, most European settlement in the region that would eventually become North Carolina was in the lowlands between the Great Dismal Swamp and Albemarle Sound. By the time of the 1663 charter, which split Carolina from Virginia, about 500 whites, mostly subsistence farmers, "undesirables" from Virginia, runaway slaves, former indentured servants, religious dissenters, and debtors lived in the region with a small number of slaves. Whereas wealthy planters dominated government and society in Virginia and later in South Carolina, the people of the Albemarle were mostly small farmers of modest means who owned their own land.

Although the native tribes of northeastern North Carolina were in decline by the 1680s, before 1711 about 30,000 Tuscarora and Algonquian people remained in the region, and they often sold land directly to early white settlers. A 1672 pact with the Tuscarora stipulated that whites could only settle north of the Albemarle Sound—an agreement overturned through war and treachery. Where other white settlers resolutely subjugated blacks and Indians, Albemarle residents were more accepting of nonwhites, and free blacks often made their homes in this region. Indians and free blacks could vote until 1715 (Barth, 2010).

A French trader remarked in 1765 on the total absence of wealthy residents, and said that many homes in the Albemarle region were so utilitarian, a simple brick chimney was considered an extravagance.

Geography impeded trade. While South Carolina and Virginia had easily accessible ports, ships arriving in North Carolina contended first with the shifting sand banks, then with the shallow sounds and widely scattered settlements behind them. At the treacherous inlets, goods were frequently transferred to and from smaller vessels. Smugglers sometimes evaded authorities in the challenging waters of North Carolina and found a lively market for ill-gotten goods among the lowland residents.

North Carolina stockmen followed the typical colonial practice of allowing their livestock free range, fencing them away from resources where they were not welcome, such as crops and gardens. Not until 1873 did the state General Assembly pass An Act Relating to Fences, which required confinement of livestock in five Piedmont counties. By 1880, all or parts of 30 or more counties were under the stock law. Residents were obliged not only to fence in their own stock, but also to fence their crops to keep out roaming livestock from nearby areas not under the stock law. In 1901 several new laws allowed natural barriers, such as rivers and thick woods, to serve as fences.

When the British Parliament imposed a tax on fences in 1670, subsistence farmers in the colonies who had not already done so were motivated to move most of their livestock to islands and peninsulas, effectively penning them by water. A peninsula required at most only a fence at some narrow spot to contain the animals, and a barrier island required no fence at all. Islands had been used for grazing since the beginning of European settlement in the New World. Eventually islands and necks all along the East Coast supported free-range livestock, including Boston Neck; Staten Island; Point Judith, Rhode Island; and many parts of Long Island. The first Georgia colonists likewise turned livestock loose in river swamps and "feeding marshes" as well as on barrier islands.

Livestock typically grazed in marshy areas considered unsuitable for any other use. John Lawson, who traveled throughout the Carolina colony in the early 1700s, before its division into North and South, observed,

> The Country in general affords pleasant Seats, the Land
> (except in some few Places) being dry and high Banks, parcell'd
> out into most convenient Necks, (by the Creeks) easy to be

Poney Penning on the Beach, near Oriental, N.C.

This postcard, produced around 1910, shows a roundup along the Neuse River near Oriental, N.C. Free-range horses and cattle still roamed much of Pamlico County and elsewhere on the mainland. These small horses appear to have Colonial Spanish characteristics and some coat colors typically found in the Banker herds. They are probably very similar to the horses originally released on the Outer Banks to graze. The ancestors of both groups probably included Chickasaw or Seminole Spanish horses. Note the high corral fence, suggesting that these small horses could jump a lesser barrier. Courtesy of University of North Carolina at Chapel Hill (*Poney* [sic] *Penning on the Beach*, ca. 1910).

> fenced in for securing their Stocks to more strict Boundaries,
> whereby, with a small trouble of fencing, almost every Man
> may enjoy, to himself, an entire Plantation, or rather Park.
> (1709, pp. 79–80)

By the 1650s, farmers and stockmen had settled on the necks along the northern margin of Albemarle Sound, and some of them may have turned livestock loose on the Banks not long afterwards. Conant, Juras, and Cothran (2012, p. 53) wrote, "Feral horses are known to have existed on these islands once the mainland was settled, primarily by Englishmen, from 1650 until the present."

After a royal charter created the Carolina colony from Virginia in 1663, Europeans began to settle on the barrier chain. Lee wrote that Sir John Colleton, one of eight Lords Proprietors, claimed Colington Island, on the west side of the Outer Banks. Colleton settled the island by proxy in 1664, when his agent Captain John Whittie "cleared a farm, planted corn, and turned cattle loose to graze" (2008, p. 51).

Not every settler was so well-connected, however:

> The land grants on the Banks during the colonial period were often very large, necessarily so for the purpose of stock raising . . . it should be remembered that the ownership represented by grants and deeds did not always mean control or occupation of the land. Presumably many of the early settlers acquired their property merely by settling on it. (Dunbar, 1958, p. 14)

These poor squatters fenced small homesteads and grew sand-tolerant vegetables such as sweet potatoes and collards on family farms. A small community of Native Americans, most likely of the same culture encountered by Verrazzano's expedition two centuries earlier, remained in the maritime forest near Cape Hatteras through the early 1700s.

"By 1680 stock had been placed on the northernmost section of the Outer Banks" (DeBlieu, 1987/1998, p. 27). Stick explained,

> It was not long before the raising of cattle, horses, hogs and sheep was an important occupation on the Banks, though most of the stock seems to have been owned by the larger, non-resident property owners. When Sir William Berkeley sold a half interest in Roanoke Island to Joshua Lamb of Massachusetts in 1676, for example, it was specifically provided that Lamb should receive half of "all the Cattle, hogs, and other stock . . . thereon," and the first attempt to survey the boundary between Virginia and Carolina in 1692 was begun "at a place called Cowpenpoint on the north side of Corotuck River, or Inlet." (1958, p. 23)

> Lee writes that early European arrivals lived in scattered settlements along the northern banks down to present-day Nags Head, below which Roanoke Inlet separated the islands. South of Roanoke Inlet a few landowners bought up large tracts, dividing nearly the entire outer banks [sic] between nine people by the early 1700s. (2008, p. 42)

Charles Felton Pidgin, a playwright and novelist from Massachusetts, described the Banker people as "distinctly strange, something of a cross between various nationalities; an unprincipled people, piratical, superstitious, uncleanly and ignorant; the substantials of life consisting of fish and wild hogs and cattle, with but scant provisions of bread and vegetables" (1907, p. 419).

The Outer Banks is one of several places known as the Graveyard of the Atlantic, having seen more than 1,000 shipwrecks since 1600. Unpredictable weather, dangerous shoals, strong currents, treacherous inlets, confusing topography, continuous change, and the late arrival of navigational aids made the place uncongenial to maritime traffic. Ships have come to grief not only on shoals, but also in deep water and on solid ground.

Legend has it that the Outer Bankers were opportunists who turned shipwrecks to their advantage. As the story goes, rather than waiting for ships to spill their cargo on the shore, the wily Bankers lured ships in to wreck on the shoals. It is said that they tied a lantern around the neck of a Banker pony and led him slowly up and down the high dunes now known as Jockeys Ridge so that the light was visible at sea. Any mariner to see the light would mistake it for a ship bobbling in a safe harbor and head for it, only to run aground. The land pirates would then loot and burn the stranded ship.

Pidgin (1907, p. 419) wrote,

> There are contradictory accounts relative to the name of this strip of sand. The early mariners say that the shore from Kitty Hawk, late the scene of the Wright brother's [sic] experiments with the flying machine, to the Oregon Inlet, presents the appearance of a nag's head, the ears made prominent by the high sand hills. Possibly this is true, but more probably may the name be accepted from the fact that the natives, a crude and lawless set of people, affixed torches on long poles, mounted their native banker ponies, and walked the beach stormy nights to allure the ships nearer the shore. This is the local acceptation; in those days there were no light-houses near, none save the stars of the universe, the light of the angels' eyes.

Dunbar (1958) disagreed with this stereotype. Like Stick (1958), he found only two instances of piracy, the looting of the grounded HMS *Hady* in 1696 and the exploitation, with outsiders, of three storm-damaged ships from the 1750 Spanish treasure fleet. Dunbar concluded, "The nature of these cases and their rarity demonstrate that the early Bankers were undeserving of their reputation as wreckers or land pirates" (1958, p. 21). More typically, Banker people took shipwreck survivors into their homes and provided whatever assistance they could.

Even if they were not of nefarious bent, Banks dwellers showed a marked tendency to resist authority. In 1750, Colonial Governor Gabriel Johnston described them as "a set of People who live on certain sandy islands lying between the Sound and the Ocean, and who are very Wild and ungovernable, so that it is seldom possible to Execute any Civil or Criminal Writs among them" (Lee, 2008, p. 49).

Popular legends hold that the original Banker horses swam to the sandy islands from the wreck of a Spanish or English ship. While this scenario is possible, there is no proof. However, trade flourished from the earliest days of the North American colonies, and many of the ships sailing the Atlantic carried horses. Wrecks were commonplace and poorly documented, and storms often swept horses off the decks where they were carried even when the ships remained intact.

Horses were shipped to and from the British colonies from the early 1600s. The horses that rode the salty swells were drawn from a relatively small gene pool, and many outwardly diverse American breeds mostly derive from the horses cultivated in this colonial nursery.

These ancestral horses descended from European, Middle Eastern, and North African animals sent to Spanish, British, French, and Dutch colonies in the New World. Many colonists who settled in Virginia and Carolina initially obtained their horses in the West Indies. Most of these animals were Spanish Jennets bred on the islands to support Spanish exploration and exploitation of the New World. New England colonists also imported stock from England, and Dutch colonists in New York got some of theirs from the Netherlands. Horses turned out to forage for themselves multiplied prodigiously, especially in New England.

Settlers on the Outer Banks fenced their yards against the predations of the abundant free-roaming livestock that had the run of the island. Each village had its own identity, often characterized by the products of local industries. Hatteras Village, "nearest to a deep and dependable inlet," was chiefly a fishing village and considered more

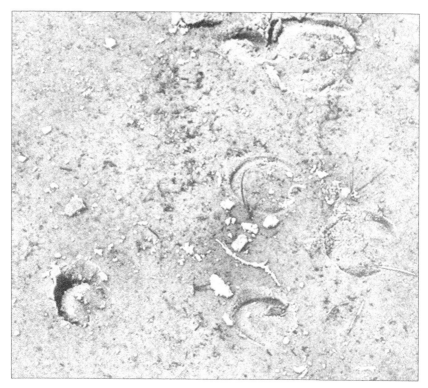

The moist sand of the intertidal zone shows a pattern of equine hoof-prints. If somehow one could hike back through the sands of time, the beach of Currituck Banks would look very similar during most of the last 400 years.

sophisticated than other Hatteras Island communities. Kinnakeet (later called Avon), was known for boat building, the harvesting of eelgrass (*Zostera marina*) for mattress stuffing, and yaupon tea.

Dunbar (1958, p. 42) wrote that by 1776 the Banks were covered with cattle, sheep, and hogs, and "the few inhabitants living on the banks (were) chiefly persons whose estates consist in livestock." Roundups were held once or twice a year to divide and brand stock and remove certain animals to the mainland. Breeding stock remained to roam freely and multiply at will. These animals were often driven up the Banks to Virginia to be sold.

In 1900, *Chambers's Journal* published a piece that reads,

> In the state of North Carolina, along the shores of the Albemarle and Pamlico Sounds, lie miles of low sandy banks, the greater part covered with little vegetation but coarse grass,

wild parsley, and other saltwater weeds. . . . On some of these banks are a breed of small wild horses, known in the neighbourhood as 'banker ponies.' They are quite untamed and uncared for, with rough shaggy coats, and are generally about twice the size of a Shetland Pony; now and again one even reaching the size of a small horse.

Each year the herd-owners drive them into pens, where the foals are branded with the owner's mark, and those required are caught and sold to the dealers who attend the annual penning. The poor things are frightfully wild and—to apply the darky term for their state—'ignorant,' and have to be starved into eating grain and hay or grass. . . .

In captivity they show equal intelligence, though seldom a reliable temper. They are tamed by darkness and semi-starvation, and make excellent draught animals, showing strength far beyond their size. They also eat voraciously, consuming as much as a full-sized horse.

The foals bred from 'banker ponies' in captivity make valuable though small horses. They are strong, healthy, and intelligent, less vicious than their parents, and command good prices. One mare used for some years by the writer as a saddle-horse was sold for thirty pounds—a good price in those parts; her sire and dam had cost respectively two and three pounds. She was a pretty little animal, could open any ordinary fastening with her teeth, and was frequently found with her head in the feed-bin. ("Fishing Horses," p. 493)

A *Washington Post* article after the turn of last century likened them to Chincoteague ponies, which at that time were similarly colored:

Currituck Sound has a race of ponies much like those of Chincoteague. They are not literally wild horses, since they have owners, and the colts are branded. The natives of the region use them for ordinary domestic purposes and the largest of the breed very well serve the needs of their owners.

Like the Chincoteague ponies, they are easily kept, and on the whole they furnish cheap horses for the poor farmers of the coast. The Chincoteague ponies can be bought at auction upon the island for $40 or $50 [roughly $1,000–$1,250 today,

Corolla

and the Currituks are probably cheaper. ("Chincoteague Ponies," 1905, p. 6)

Marvin Howard of Ocracoke (1976, p. 26) gave this description:

> The ponies of the Outer Banks did vary in weight from five hundred to eight hundred pounds. They lived on the range the year round as wild as deer or wild horses can ever be. For sustenance they had only the salt grass, the boughs of live oak and red cedar, and when the winters were severe, they dug in the sand hills with their hoofs to get the succulent roots of the sea oats. These ponies no doubt had strains of Arab steed for in numbers of them there was untold beauty in color and build. They were fleet of feet, hardy, well lined, and full of muscle. . . . None of these wild horses were ever large except the Pea Island pony, which came from the original quarter-bred horse.

A persistent legend holds that the horses of the Outer Banks were directly established by Spanish explorers through either shipwreck or colonization attempts. It is, however, unlikely that any Spanish horses brought to the East Coast of North America in the 1500s made it this far north or stayed long enough to leave progeny.

Farming was very small-scale—Bankers maintained small kitchen gardens beside their homes, fenced to keep the livestock out. Windmills ground corn that fishermen obtained in trade from mainland farmers.

In the early days, communities were usually established on the more protected mainland, leaving the Banks largely to livestock. The Banks were low and grassy, with wide beaches, scattered dunes to the west, and forested areas on the soundside. Over time, pilots and other watermen settled near the inlets, and villages were established in the parts of the islands stabilized by maritime forest. By the early 1800s, seasonal visitors began building cottages on the soundside. Hotels and other establishments followed. The first substantial oceanfront structure on the northern Banks was built in Nags Head just before the Civil War. After 1900, vacationers built cottages near the sea and moved them westward as the beach receded.

Oddly enough, commercial fishing was not a primary occupation or source of income on the Banks through the first two centuries of settlement. The 1850 census showed that fishing was the primary occupation on Hatteras Island, but commercial fishermen were in the minority on Portsmouth and Ocracoke. At that time, many mainland dwellers still lived close to waters that teemed with fish, so there was little incentive for them to import seafood from the Outer Banks.

This dynamic shifted abruptly between the Civil War and World War II, when Bankers turned to the sea and sound, not just to live, but also to make a living. They sold not only fish, but also porpoises, turtles (diamondback terrapins and loggerhead and green turtles), clams, scallops, oysters, crabs, waterfowl, and eelgrass.

Whales had been hunted off the coast of North Carolina since 1666. A porpoise fishery operated in Hatteras from the late 1700s until the Civil War. Watermen would trap and process entire pods of dolphins, including pregnant and lactating females and nursing calves, strip them of blubber, render the oil, and discard the flesh and skin. Up to 1,200 animals were taken in a season, and five or six porpoises could be processed into one barrel of oil. During the 1800s, free-roaming swine on Hatteras Island feasted on the scraps that remained after this butchery. Porpoise oil was burned in lamps and used in soapmaking, and from 1844 until around 1970 refined oil from the "melon" (an echolocation organ) was the favored lubricant for watches, clocks, and other delicate mechanisms. The Hatteras fishery harvested porpoises until about the early 1900s.

Loggerhead turtles were speared or tackled by fishermen who dived overboard onto the reptiles, turned their heads upward, and muscled them to shore. Eventually, the federal government stepped in to protect sea turtles from extinction.

Tourism and related development, now the economic underpin-ning of the Outer Banks, began on Ocracoke and around Nags Head before the Civil War. Because there were no roads, the mostly regional clientele arrived by steamer or private boat. The soundside at Nags Head soon had a hotel, a cluster of vacation houses, and docks up to a half mile (0.8 km) long, some supporting rails on which horses or oxen hauled wealthy visitors and their summer's baggage.

Battles and shipwrecks drew attention to the Banks, but the Wright brothers thrust the area permanently into the national limelight on December 17, 1903, when they made the first controlled flights in a self-propelled heavier-than-air machine near Kill Devil Hill. They had first visited three years earlier, after searching by mail for windy spots

In the time of the Wright brothers, Kitty Hawk appeared a veritable desert of barren, windblown dunes (Daniels, 1903). Courtesy of Library of Congress.

where they could experiment in privacy. Kitty Hawk postmaster William J. Tate (1900) wrote back, "our winds are always steady" and "you will find a hospitable people." His description of the terrain, flat and treeless in many places and free of rocks, may have sweetened the deal: "You could for instance get a stretch of sandy land 1 mile by five with a bare hill in center 80 feet high not a tree or bush anywhere to break the evenness of the wind."

At the time of the Wright Brothers' experiments, most of the Outer Banks were low, windswept dunes with wide beaches to the east and marsh and maritime forest to the west. For centuries, experts and laymen alike harbored the misconception that the banks were heavily forested before the arrival of Europeans. Engraver Theodor De Bry (1590) apparently added trees to John White's original maps, giving the false impression of forestation. Spears (1890) imagined the virginal Hatteras Island as "almost completely covered with a prodigious growth of trees" (p. 510). He blamed the change, and the sand wave burying the island, on overzealous logging.

The dense, heavy wood of live oaks (*Quercus* spp.) was favored in shipbuilding, but they were depleted before the Civil War, Harvesting of loblolly pine (*Pinus taeda*) in Buxton Woods started in 1899. From 1907 to 1911, the Foreman-Blades Lumber Company of Elizabeth City, N.C., aggressively logged parts of Hatteras Island, mostly cutting loblolly pine, oak, holly (*Ilex* spp.), and dogwood (*Cornus florida*) 8 in./20 cm or greater in diameter. It spared the largest trees, many of which later succumbed to insect infestations. A sawmill on the soundside in Nags Head processed trees from Nags Head Woods, and loggers cleared enough of what is now Southern Shores and Kitty Hawk to warrant a short narrow-gauge railroad ending at a sawmill on Kitty Hawk Bay.

Most of the islands' woodlands have recovered from the removal of old-growth trees in previous centuries and show few signs of exploitation. Logging, accidental and deliberately set fires, and land clearing, however, apparently have altered the composition of the maritime forest. Between roughly 900 and 170 years ago, Buxton Woods was 51% oak and 30% pine. The balance began to shift around 1700. In 1987, Buxton Woods was 6% oak and 80% pine.

Around the beginning of the 20th century, persuasive commentators blamed free-roaming livestock, at least in part, for denuding the Banks. For example, Jay Bond of the U.S. Forest Service wrote (1908, p. 43) that hogs turned up the soil and exposed the roots of grasses, which cattle and sheep devoured, creating a "blowout" that could form a destructive sand wave. Bond recommended driving rows of planks into the ground to catch wind-borne sand; planting sea oats (*Uniola paniculata*) to hold the sand in place and catch more; and planting loblolly pines behind the artificial dune line to reestablish the forest. He also recommended forcing owners to fence in their livestock. His ideas took root a generation later.

Collier Cobb, a geology professor at the University of North Carolina, shared Bond's belief that the islands could be stabilized. He proposed "reforesting the sands" by systematic planting (1906, p. 317), which he said would turn Hatteras Island into "a subtropical garden." Cobb, however, did not see free-roaming horses as a problem, and he speculated that with the plantings, "the herds of wild ponies now dwindling away would again increase in numbers."

At the time, people did not understand barrier island dynamics. Now scientists realize that barrier islands are inherently unstable, with or without logging or livestock. Dunes appear to go through stages of migration that have little to do with human activity. They mobilize, engulfing and killing forests as overwash and the winds of nor'easters push them across the island. Then they restabilize when colonized

A live dune on Cumberland Island National Seashore engulfs and kills vegetation in its path. Sand dunes periodically mobilize and migrate, then stabilize and revegetate, a natural process that cannot be duplicated with earth-moving equipment and plantings.

by plants that form soil. Sometimes the dunes of the Outer Banks became mountains of sand much higher than the trees they smothered, reaching over 90 ft/27 m. The town of Seagull (later renamed Old Inlet) stood at the base of Penny Hill until the migrating dune completely buried the village in the 1950s.

By radiocarbon-dating the soil, geologists concluded that the large dunes on Currituck Banks have been live and migratory from 750 to 1000 CE, from 1260 to 1700, and from around 1830 to the present. There is also indirect evidence that sand waves on Hatteras Island pre-dated European contact. If Hatorask, on the 1590 White-De Bry map, comes from the Algonquian for "there is less vegetation" (Quinn, 1955, p. 864), it suggests sparse plant cover. Chicamacomico, an Algonquian-derived name for a cape at the north end of Hatteras Island, may mean "sinking-down sand" (Quinn, 1955, p. 864), which implies erosion or dune migration. In the late 16th century, this cape evidently had dunes and a maritime forest. Less than a century later, the cape was gone, replaced by Wimble Shoals and a bend in the coastline. Its rapid disappearance may have been part of changes that began centuries before the Raleigh colonists arrived.

A pair of Banker Horses threads a maze of sand fences employed to slow the attrition of the primary dunes. In some places on Currituck Banks, natural dunes are in a "live" migratory phase, to the vexation of developers. Many blame free-roaming horses for destabilizing the dunes, but dune migration is an inevitable process.

Not all islands develop high dunes. On a natural barrier island, influences such as sand supply and transport and the direction of the prevailing winds give some areas a surplus of sand, resulting in higher dunes. Other islands, including most parts of the Outer Banks, naturally develop low dunes, wide beaches, and overwash flats. For example, sea-floor sediments 40 ft/12 m below the ocean surface determine the profile of Shackleford Banks. Where the nearby ocean floor is thick sand, Shackleford has high dunes. Where it is rocky with little sand, Shackleford has overwash flats.

Under natural conditions, grasses can establish themselves on the dunes within a season. Sea oats grow in clusters, and between them, gaps form in the sandbanks that let fingers of sandy overwash probe the hollows. Once grasses stabilize a dune line, other plants can follow, though it may take a decade or two for shrubs to take hold and centuries to grow a maritime forest.

Dunes on Shackleford Banks stopped migrating sometime between 1917 and 1939, during an interval with fewer severe storms. From

1939 to 1971, sea-oat and scrub thicket cover expanded; the dune fields revegetated spontaneously despite the presence of large herds of free-roaming horses, cattle, sheep, goats, and hogs.

Photographs taken from the top of the Cape Hatteras Lighthouse in the 1920s show wide beaches and, behind them, a lightly vegetated overwash flat roughly 200 yards/183 m wide. These flats and beaches were important nesting habitat for native birds. Despite the presence of thousands of head of livestock, the island topography appeared to have changed very little over 300 years. Spared further human interference, it might have maintained this state indefinitely.

The Wright brothers last flew on the Banks in 1911, but their local legacy endured. As the 25th anniversary of aviation approached, W.O. Saunders, an Elizabeth City newspaper editor, and others prodded the federal government to erect a national monument atop Kill Devil Hill, near the site of the first successful flight. In 1928, Coast Guardsmen, residents, and paid workers planted vegetation and removed free-roaming livestock in hopes of anchoring the massive dune. Eventually the government mounted a 60-ft./18-m granite pylon at its apex. Completion of the monument in 1931 seemed to prove that impressive feats of stabilization were possible.

The Wright *Flyer* put the Outer Banks on the map, but it was the horseless carriage that made it a national resort. As automobiles became popular, adventurous visitors sometimes drove down the beach from Virginia or brought their cars to the Banks via private ferry. By 1925, Roanoke Island had a paved road, and 13 Hatteras Islanders owned automobiles. In 1927, after state engineers had declared that the Banks would need no road or bridge for "fifty years or more" (Stick, 1958, p. 244), Dare County Commissioner Washington Baum boldly started work on bridges and a causeway connecting Roanoke Island and Nags Head. Envisioning the automobile as a key to prosperity, he started this project without permission or funding at a time when few people owned automobiles and there were no paved roads on the Outer Banks.

The awkwardly-named Kill Devil Hill Monument National Memorial, near the site of the Wrights' first flight, drew visitors, and the expectation of more tourism justified expenditures for new roads and bridges. The privately operated 3-mi/4.8-km Wright Brothers Memorial Bridge, completed in 1930, granted vehicles access from the mainland. By 1931, it was possible to drive from the Currituck County mainland to Kitty Hawk, follow the new paved highway to Nags Head, and cross the bridge and causeway to Manteo. In 1932, the state of North Carolina assumed responsibility for maintaining all this new infrastructure. Investors from Elizabeth City and Norfolk eagerly built service stations, hotels, and restaurants on the newly accessible real estate.

These entrepreneurs based their dreams on an unstable barrier chain, and disaster was sure to follow. In 1933 alone, two hurricanes and a number of lesser storms flattened dunes and dwellings and breached or buried the new blacktop. Economic development, which had become imperative with the coming of the Great Depression, depended on preserving and extending the highway, which depended on stabilizing not just one hill, but the whole beach. The same year, the state Department of Conservation and Development proposed the North Carolina Coastal Development Project, which involved building dunes, restoring the banks to their "primal heavily forested condition," paving a Hatteras Island highway, and establishing a national coastal park (Senter, 2003).

In the early 1900s, while Bond and Cobb pondered stabilizing the Banks, H.C. Cowles of the University of Chicago introduced the concept of ecological succession, which became central to the emerging science of plant ecology. An ecosystem endures by maintaining a balance among interdependent species. These species make way for different species until a balanced ecosystem forms. For example, a meadow may emerge from a wetland, support the growth of shrubs and trees, and eventually turn into a forest. As succession progresses, the community becomes more diverse and the total mass of its organisms increases. Ultimately, the ecosystem reaches a climax, a balanced state of maximal biodiversity and biomass. Cowles compared the climax community to the adult stage of an organism. It persists until, inevitably, some cataclysm such as a fire begins the process of secondary succession.

Stages of succession do not necessarily occur in a particular order, though, and sometimes species appear randomly and establish themselves in favorable conditions. Pioneer species change the environment, primarily by soil formation, and make it suitable for the plants that will replace them.

Sometimes succession occurs in response to climate change over millennia. Sometimes it occurs more quickly because the species within the ecosystem change the habitat with their presence. When grasses take root in open water, the ecosystem shifts to marsh. Some systems are beset so frequently by disturbances—fires, floods, over-grazing—that a climax community never appears.

These environmental dynamics were poorly understood in the early 20th century. Prevailing theories held that biological systems move inexorably "toward an unchanging plateau of stability where they will remain until their 'natural balance' is disturbed by, for example, human-induced deforestation" (Binkley, 2007, p. 201). Many feared that the deforestation of the Outer Banks caused shoreline erosion, an irrevocable loss of land that would end in the disappearance of the islands. In the 1930s, scientists, engineers, and politicians touted artificial dune construction as the way to save the Banks by artificially returning it to its "natural" state.

Between 1933 and 1940, the Civilian Conservation Corps, under direction of the Works Progress Administration and later the Park Service, installed more than 3 million ft (568 mi/914 km) of sand fencing in parallel rows to catch sand and build dunes as high as 25 ft/7.6 m, with bases nearly 300 ft/91 m across. This project planted 142 million ft^2 (3,260 acres/1,319 ha) of dune grasses and more than 2.5 million trees and shrubs along 115 mi/185 km of North Carolina coast. It laid the foundation for what was thought to be restoration of the prehistoric landscape.

Although the livestock industry was winding down, several thousand horses, cattle, sheep, goats, and swine still roamed the Banks. Some considered them a threat to beach stabilization and economic development. Advocates of wildlife refuges and a national seashore likewise considered them a threat to the natural balance of native species. MacNeill saw them as a health hazard. "Extinction of these wild cattle and ponies has been long advocated as a health measure. The cattle are virtually useless, and useful herds have died out of disease as soon as they were introduced" (MacNeill, 1938, p. 1).

In 1935, the North Carolina General Assembly passed legislation that required livestock owners to fence their animals. Two years later, lawmakers extended the stock law to Currituck Banks. Most affected stockmen did not own large tracts of land, and their animals

"One of the great dunes at Kitty Hawk, anchored with brush fence and coarse grass" (Farrell, n.d.). The recent-looking plantings must have been made after the state proposed large-scale beach stabilization in 1933. Damage to the new highway in the foreground—note the water-filled gully and broken blacktop—may be from the hurricane of August 23 or September 15, 1933; the hurricane of September 8, 1934; or any of several nor'easters. Photograph courtesy of the State Archives of North Carolina.

traditionally grazed in marsh and woods owned by neighbors, hunt clubs, or absentees. They lacked the resources to maintain stock profitably on their own property. Suddenly families comprising generations of herders were forced to find another livelihood. Within a few years, the number of large livestock operations on the Outer Banks shrank from about 50 to seven or eight. The days of free-roaming herds north of Ocracoke had officially ended.

In 1938, two local men equipped with "high-powered rifles and dum-dum bullets" methodically gunned down most of the remaining unfenced livestock in Dare County—"about 100 wild cows and upwards of 50 wild ponies" plus swine (MacNeill, 1938, p. 1). County officials paid the hunters a bounty of $5 a head, roughly $82 today. MacNeill (1958) reported that First Lady Eleanor Roosevelt's younger brother Hall Roosevelt killed the last unfenced cow on Hatteras Island, apparently for sport, and gave the bounty away. Yet despite the sweeping eradication of domestic stock, small herds of horses remained on the islands below Hatteras Inlet and on the northern reaches of Currituck Banks.

By the late 1960s, ecologists began to realize that natural systems must constantly shift and adapt to changing environmental forces and can only remain "stable" under conditions that allow change. Natural dune systems maintain a state of dynamic stability, responding to changes in wave energy, water level, and sediment supply with continual changes in configuration. Tsoar (2005) concluded that the main stressor limiting dune vegetation is erosion by wind.

Whereas the overwash passes and dunefields of a natural shoreface absorb the energy of storm-driven waves, the roiling ocean slams into continuous artificial dunes with full intensity. Waves erode the dune-line and carry sand offshore, gradually narrowing the beach. Artificial dunes, jetties, groins, buildings, and other structures throw the system perpetually out of balance, so people must intervene to solve one problem after another. The beach erodes, so they add more sand. The dunes breach, so they rebuild them. A house, a business, a road washes away, so they rebuild to the west.

Noting "how stabilization has changed the morphology and ecology of the beaches, dunes, and marshes," Dolan and Lins (1987, p. 76) wrote, "The paradox suggests that manmade structures do not merely fail to protect beaches but actually work to destroy them." Moreover, shoreline development, beach stabilization, and heavy use by off-road vehicles degrade habitats and have contributed to the decline of a long list of rare species. The National Park Service gave up on dune stabilization in the early 1970s because of maintenance costs and negative geological and ecological effects.

DeKimpe, Dolan & Hayden (1991) noted that beaches 328–410 ft/100–125 m wide before stabilization shrank to 230–328 ft/70–100 m by the mid-1940s and to an average of 39 m/128 ft by the early 1990s, when some were as narrow as 33 ft/10 m. The effects of stabilization, however, are not limited to the beach. Jockeys Ridge, the largest sand dune on the East Coast, has decreased in height from 138 ft/42 m above sea level in 1953 to 110 ft/33.5 m in 1974 and 87.5 ft/26.7 m in 1995, probably because of stabilization of the surrounding area. The natural flow of sand is disrupted by artificial dunes, buildings, and opportunistic vegetation. Centuries of free-roaming livestock had little impact, but stabilization has caused rapid deterioration.

On Currituck Banks, largely ignored by officials and developers until the mid-1970s, horses survived. The small herd spent little

Sand fences catch sand and build dunes, but the resulting sand hills are more fragile than those built by natural processes.

time in the company of people, but when horses did wander into a village, they peacefully coexisted with the residents, who maintained deep emotional ties with them. A minimally manipulated line of natural dunes backed by maritime forest extends from Corolla north to the Virginia line. This area is essential to the survival of both free-roaming horses and the barrier chain. Spreading live oaks and other trees provide shelter during hurricanes, and their root systems hold soil in place when overwash sweeps the island. This and other maritime forests are the least stabilized, therefore most stable, parts of the barrier chain.

Corolla is the only survivor of several settlements in the area that developed around Lifesaving Service stations established in the 1870s. Three others also had post offices with unrelated names. Wash Woods lost its post office (Deals) in 1917, but had enough residents to remain a voting precinct in Virginia Beach until 1966.

Most of the other settlements on Currituck Banks were tiny and short-lived. The town of Seagull (later called Old Inlet) may have dated back to the days of commerce through New Currituck Inlet, which opened in the hurricane of 1713 and persisted after the 1730 closure of Old Currituck Inlet. Around the turn of the 19th century, the new inlet closed, along with Caffeys and Roanoke inlets to the south, causing a downturn in the shipping and fishing trades. Stock raising and subsistence farming continued, however, and the freshening of Currituck Sound caused a dramatic increase in populations of migratory waterfowl. After the Civil War, wealthy Northern sportsmen and local market gunners slaughtered waterfowl until populations collapsed and Congress outlawed commercial hunting in 1918. At its peak, this village had 35 houses, some of them occupied by families of the crew at Penny's Hill Lifesaving Station; two churches; a one-room school; and, from 1908 to 1924, a post office.

When Penny Hill migrated in the 1950s, the village was smothered under the giant dune. The Ash Wednesday Storm, a devastating nor'easter, reopened New Currituck Inlet in 1962, and destroyed part of the dune, and federal and state agencies used some of the remaining sand hill to fill the breach.

The village of Corolla was originally called Whales Head, and then renamed Currituck Beach. When the post office opened in 1895, it was named Corolla. Eventually the name stuck on the little unincorporated town. Corolla was difficult to reach by land, but readily accessible by water.

In 1925, Edward Knight of Philadelphia, an industrialist who made his fortune primarily from the Pennsylvania Railroad and the American Sugar refinery, and his wife, Marie Louise Knight, completed the Whalehead Club, an opulent 21,000 ft^2/1,951 m^2 home in the Art

On Currituck Banks, Penny (more correctly Lewark) Hill provides horses and other wildlife high ground during floods. The extinct village of Seagull lies smothered beneath this massive dune.

Nouveau style. There they maintained their privileged lifestyle and hunted the abundance of fowl that wintered on Currituck Banks.

In 1939, shortly after it had absorbed the Lighthouse Service, the the U.S. Coast Guard dismissed the Currituck Beach Lighthouse keeper and automated the light. It ran on batteries charged by a generator till the Virginia Electric and Power Company ran lines to Corolla in 1955. Until 1973, the only land access from the south was by 15 mi/24 km of rutty, unpaved state road. Alternatively, one could use the beach, driving between the high and low tidemarks, but for the inexperienced this was often an unreliable and risky means of travel.

In 1973, developers paved a road from the Dare County line north to near the village, but restricted access until 1984. While access to Corolla from the south was limited, the Fish and Wildlife Service blocked access from the north through Back Bay National Wildlife Refuge. Many Corolla residents and nonresident property owners found it difficult to leave or return legally. They railed against the restrictions with petitions and public hearings, and ultimately a child died when access to medical attention was unnecessarily delayed. In the 1980s, developers to the south of Corolla shifted their focus from maintaining exclusivity to accommodating tourists.

When the state took over responsibility for maintaining the road in 1984, the outside world descended on the little village. Beautiful Corolla was secluded no longer. In 1985, there were only 35 full-time residents. A decade later, that number had more than tripled, but the bulk of the population influx came from thousands of people eager to rent seasonal beach homes or just visit for the day.

Magazines and billboards touted Corolla as an "undiscovered paradise," and people came flocking to the "empty beaches" to soak up the solitude. Cars zoomed around the bends of Highway 12. Condominiums sprang up like the lesions of a fast-breeding virus. Price tags were high, but there was no shortage of wealthy vacationers eager to buy into this new retreat. The juxtaposition of sleek wild horses and expensive condominiums, nature and progress, inspired an emotionally charged war with powerful opinions on either side.

Free-roaming horses are strongly motivated to stay within their home ranges throughout their lives. Survival increases when they know which food source is available with the season, where to find water, and where to escape floods or biting insects. When developers placed a beach cottage or housing complex within this home range, the horses coped as best they could and foraged around the new obstacles. They had few options. The surrounding ranges were already claimed by other horse bands that would fight to repel intruders.

The dark horses that often crossed the road at night knew nothing about the impatient, lead-footed drivers that flew down the new roadways. By 1989, 17 horses had been killed in road accidents, six of them in a single incident. Residents and visitors united to create the Corolla Wild Horse Fund. Their mission was to guard the Corolla horses against the human invasion and attempt to preserve their wildness.

The horses needed government protection, but they were ineligible because government agencies deemed them not native or not wildlife. Hunt clubs complained that they ate the food planted for the waterfowl and asked the North Carolina Wildlife Resources Commission to remove the herd, but the horses were not considered native wildlife and were therefore not its concern. Currituck County looked to the state for help. The state bounced responsibility back to the county.

As Corolla residents wrestled with red tape, horses died on the highway. The Corolla Wild Horse Fund outfitted the horses with reflective collars to make them more visible to motorists, sprayed

Through the 1990s, numerous signs along Highway 12 warned motorists of the wild horses in the road, but fatalities occurred regularly. In this case, it appears that a driver had run over the sign. Other visitors stole the signs as souvenirs, leaving the horses unprotected.

their bodies with glow-in-the-dark paint, and posted signs along Highway 12 warning motorists to slow down because of "horses on road at any time." These tactics helped to reduce, but not eliminate fatalities. Vacationers even stole some signs as souvenirs.

The fatalities were devastating. In 1990, a mare known as Bay Girl delivered her long-anticipated foal, who was to be named Freedom. The day after his birth, the newborn was found floating in a pond with the umbilical cord still attached. The wounds on his little body told

A stallion inspects a newly constructed beach house in 1995, unfazed by the loud hammering of nearby carpenters working to complete the next house in the fast-growing complex.

In the mid-1990s, a mare grazed in the driveway of a beach house off Highway 12 in Corolla. When developers built housing complexes within the home ranges of the horses, the animals adapted.

The author took this photograph looking northeast from the top of the Currituck Beach Lighthouse in the late 1990s, well after the development boom had begun.

Same view, taken in 2012.

View to the southeast of the lighthouse, 2012.

the story—someone had hit him with a car and then thrown him into the water. Bay Girl's previous foal had also been killed by a vehicle.

Star, a black patriarch with a white star on his forehead, was a magnificent animal, the leader of a 23-member band. A photograph gracing the cover of *Outer Banks Magazine* showed him prancing down the beach, neck arched, a powerful animal in the prime of life. Star's son Midnight constantly fought his father for possession of the band, or at least a few of the mares. Their battles were frequent and intense. Midnight eventually acquired a mare from the north ranges, but returned to steal more from Star.

In May 1991, Star forced Midnight into a hasty retreat, which took the two battle-crazed stallions across a road at a gallop. Midnight made it across safely, but Star was hit by a fast-moving vehicle and killed. After witnessing the highway deaths of three of his mares and seven of his foals, Star joined the growing list of fatalities. Star was the 20th horse struck between 1985 and 1995. Midnight took over the band, but did not have the talent or experience to manage it. Other studs stole mares, and by 1993 the band was split into four.

In 1989, Currituck County adopted an ordinance that designated all of Currituck Banks a wild horse sanctuary. This made it unlawful for "any person to lure, attract, or entice a wild horse to come within 50 feet of any person" (*Currituck Outer Banks Wild Horse Management Plan*, n.d., p. 2) and protected the horses against trapping, taking, tormenting, injuring, or killing. In June 1995, Secretary Betty McCain of the North Carolina Department of Cultural Resources proclaimed, "The Corolla Wild Horses are one of North Carolina's most significant historic and cultural resources of the coastal area" (*Currituck Outer Banks Wild Horse Management Plan*, n.d., p. 3).

The county makes equine management decisions jointly with The Wild Horse Advisory Board, composed of representatives from the Corolla Wild Horse Fund, the Fish and Wildlife Service, the National Estuarine Research Reserve, along with two citizen representatives. In 1994, Currituck County and the Corolla Wild Horse Fund assigned a management agreement that designated the Fund as the lead advisor in protecting the horses.

Currituck County officials assembled members of the Wild Horse Fund, the Currituck NWR, and the Currituck NCNERR to work out a 13-point management plan. As a result, federal and state agencies have incorporated the Currituck horses into their operations. Management practices now include maintaining a herd of fewer than 60 individuals; blocking wild horse access to the developed areas in North Carolina and Virginia and relocating horses that frequent populated areas; supervising their numbers and health status, maintaining enclosures for a few horses at the Whalehead Club or the Currituck Beach Lighthouse; and using private pasturage within the off-road area.

In a small herd like the one on Currituck Banks, it is important to maintain as much genetic variety as possible in order to avoid inbreeding. Sometimes this necessity is at odds with practicality. At one point, a large percentage of foals born happened to be male, and as they grew older, they presented a unique problem.

Usually colts are driven from the herd when they reach puberty. They form bachelor bands and keep one another company until about age 5 or 6, when they are mature enough to start their own bands. Lured by the lushness of lawns in Corolla, the Currituck colts had no incentive to head north to eat marsh grass. The youngsters stayed, chasing mares around in adolescent ardor and exhausting the mature stallions, which were compelled to continually interpose themselves between the mares and the competition.

These colts ranged mostly in populated areas, and once they matured, there was sure to be intense fighting over the few available mares. Unaware tourists would surely get caught in the struggles. In 1990, the Corolla Wild Horse Fund proposed to geld bachelor colts, hoping that harem stallions would tolerate the young males if they no longer competed for reproductive rights.

This approach was controversial. Gelding would reduce the genes available for future generations. And what if something unfortunate happened to the herd stallions? The colts would then be the only hope for the continuity of bloodlines. With so many fatalities, this was certainly a concern. Opponents of the plan reasoned that wild horses should live without human intervention, beneficial or detrimental, and a gelding is not a truly wild horse. The proposal to geld was defeated.

Aggressive attempts at public education did not adequately protect the horses. While most visitors respected the ordinances, some were incredibly reckless. The same vacationers that might be a little nervous mounting a well-trained rental horse for an amble down the incorporated the Currituck horses into their operations. Management practices now include maintaining a herd of fewer than 60 individuals; blocking wild horse access to the developed areas in North Carolina and Virginia and relocating horses that frequent populated areas; supervising their numbers and health status, maintaining enclosures for a few horses at the Whalehead Club or the Currituck Beach Lighthouse; and using private pasturage within the off-road area.

In a small herd like the one on Currituck Banks, it is important to maintain as much genetic variety as possible in order to avoid inbreeding. Sometimes this necessity is at odds with practicality. At one point, a large percentage of foals born happened to be male, and as they grew older, they presented a unique problem.

Usually colts are driven from the herd when they reach puberty. They form bachelor bands and keep one another company until about age 5 or 6, when they are mature enough to start their own bands. Lured by the lushness of lawns in Corolla, the Currituck colts had no incentive to head north to eat marsh grass. The youngsters stayed, chasing mares around in adolescent ardor and exhausting the mature stallions, which were compelled to continually interpose themselves between the mares and the competition.

These colts ranged mostly in populated areas, and once they matured, there was sure to be intense fighting over the few available mares. Unaware tourists would surely get caught in the struggles. In 1990, the Corolla Wild Horse Fund proposed to geld bachelor colts, hoping that harem stallions would tolerate the young males if they no longer competed for reproductive rights.

This approach was controversial. Gelding would reduce the genes available for future generations. And what if something unfortunate happened to the herd stallions? The colts would then be the only hope for the continuity of bloodlines. With so many fatalities, this was certainly a concern. Opponents of the plan reasoned that wild horses should live without human intervention, beneficial or detrimental, and a gelding is not a truly wild horse. The proposal to geld was defeated.

Aggressive attempts at public education did not adequately protect the horses. While most visitors respected the ordinances, some were incredibly reckless. The same vacationers that might be a little nervous mounting a well-trained rental horse for an amble down the

In 2012, the Corolla Wild Horse Fund rescued a curious young horse that ascended a flight of stairs and was unable to get down. It also rescued one horse who got a tomato cage stuck on its head and neck, potentially life threatening—or blinding—for the horse. Photographs courtesy of the Corolla Wild Horse Fund.

beach actually felt safe in putting their children on the backs of these unbroken, unpredictable horses for photographs!

Unnecessary human contact eventually habituates much of the "wild" out of these horses by altering natural behavior. It can instigate aggression between horses as they squabble over proffered food. It can result in injury when the horse bites the hand that feeds it, or worse. Overly close contact can expose the visitor to vectors which carry diseases such as Lyme and encephalitis.

County ordinance required people to stay 50 ft/15 m from the horses—that is about the length of one and a half school buses. Too many tourists came in close to feed and pet them when they thought nobody was watching. Reports of kicks and bites were common.

People also did not stop to consider that a horse's digestive system is adapted to native grass. The animals may like the taste of pickles or peanut butter and jelly, but human food can make them very sick. Many well-meaning tourists fed the horses whatever was handy. Some even left plastic bags of apples and carrots out on their trashcans as treats for the horses. The animals did not understand that the bag was not intended to be part of the meal and consumed the entire offering, unaware that intestinal blockage was likely afterwards.

Domestic horses are prone to colic, but Banker Horses rarely develop digestive problems on their diet of grasses. When the horses were left to themselves, the rare instances of colic were usually due to sand ingestion. Once tourists appeared on the scene, colic became frequent and sometimes claimed lives.

One tourist actually lured a curious 2-year-old colt up onto the deck of a beach house with food. The animal fell and was almost killed. One woman trailered her mare to Corolla, hoping to breed her to a wild stallion, and exposed the herd to disease.

A normal horse, acting the way its instincts have commanded over millions of years of evolution, was justified in biting, kicking, or flattening the intruders. Horses are at their moodiest during the breeding season, which coincides with the tourist season.

Our society often has no sympathy for an animal being true to its nature. People want to interact with wildlife, and they are willing to cross boundaries and break rules to do it. They feed the Yellowstone bears. They pet the moose calf on the Vermont roadside. Wild animals accustomed to the presence of humans may appear docile, but remain

The sea-to-sound fence has been mostly effective in keeping horses north of Corolla Village, but a few enterprising horses have found their ways around the barrier.

unpredictable and can revert to dangerous instinctive behavior when stressed. Despite common sense and frequent press coverage, people are astonished and angry when the bear mauls, the moose charges, or the horse kicks. They demand retribution, and officials often typically inclined to hold the animal accountable. Animals that injure people are frequently destroyed, whether or not the action was appropriate from the animal's perspective.

Corolla Wild Horse Fund volunteers donated incalculable time to locating the herds and following nearby to keep tourists at a distance. But these volunteers had jobs and families vying for their attention, and there were too few of them to avert all potential tragedies.

In September 1994, the Wild Horse Fund attempted to block equine access to the heavily developed part of Corolla by building a fence from sea to sound at the North Beach Access ramp at the north end of N.C. 12. At first, the horses easily circumvented the fence and returned to their home ranges.

In 1995 the Fund completed an improved barrier reaching well out into the water to keep the horses north of town. It took two days to herd the horses beyond the fence, where they joined other bands that ranged as far north as Back Bay NWR in Virginia. Some observers scoffed at the fence, asserting that it would not deter horses known for their swimming ability. The average depth of Currituck Sound is only 5 ft/1.5 m, and few areas exceed 10 ft/3 m. Any enterprising horse, they argued, would easily find a way around.

Butterscotch, an ingenious lead mare, proved them right by persistently circumventing the sound side of the fence, leading her group back to the lush vegetation of the golf courses and green sod lawns. In one remarkable incident, she traveled north until she found a sandbar that extended out into the sound and reached 1,500 ft/450 m beyond the end of the fence. She and her friends sloshed through a length of foot-deep (30 cm) water and reentered Corolla well south of the barrier.

This adventure resulted in the death of Grecko, her black yearling son, in June 1995. Grecko wandered onto Highway 12 around 2 a.m. and was thrown 91 ft/28 m when struck by a vehicle. The 18-year-old driver was charged with possession of alcohol.

Sixteen horses in four separate bands regularly came around the fence to graze where the grass was greener. The public, having heard of the roundup to keep the horses north of the developed area, often did not expect to find them still in the middle of the highway.

The volunteers were shell-shocked from watching the horses die unnecessarily and horribly. They simply did not have the time, energy, or other resources to keep them safe on their home turf. In 1996, several horses that persistently returned to Corolla were removed from the Outer Banks and adopted. The rest of the horses seemed content to stay north of the barrier, living free on the mostly undeveloped land.

Then in 1999, reports of wild horses raiding yards, trash cans, and a produce stand made the news when a stallion named Little Red Man and his herd repeatedly came around the barrier to forage in Corolla. A black mare was killed on the road in 1999, orphaning her foal. Little Red Man was relocated with his mares to a 400-acre/162-ha hunt club on Dews Island in Currituck Sound.

The Currituck herd forages on about 7,544 acres/3,053 ha of the northern beach. About 70% of their range is privately owned, and the other 30% is public land specifically set aside for native wildlife preservation by entities that do not recognize horses as indigenous species. Individuals and corporations own 4,671.35 acres/1,890 ha, the Currituck National Wildlife Refuge administers 2,495.4 acres/1,010 ha, the North Carolina National Estuarine Research Reserve holds 326.5 acres/132 ha, and the nonprofit Nature Conservancy has 51 acres/21 ha.

Rheinhardt and Rheinhardt (2004) detailed seasonal habitat use by the Corolla horses. The researchers found that in late winter, horses spent much of their time in the maritime forest to escape from the wind and spent less time than expected in the cold, windy marshes. In spring, they used all available habitats. In summer, their preferred habitat was wet grassland—wet depressions dominated by plants such as cordgrass and rushes. They avoided the dry grassland of sand flats and dunes. Freshwater is always available to the horses in Currituck Sound and in ponds, puddles, and artificial canals.

In 2002, Currituck County and the Virginia Department of Conservation and Recreation built a second sea-to-sound fence 11 mi/18 km north of the Corolla barrier along the southern boundary of False Cape State Park at the Virginia state line to restrict horses from migrating to the developed areas of Virginia. Horses sometimes find their way through, around, or over this fence to range into the Back Bay NWR, where they graze on developing waterfowl food plants within impoundments. The public enjoys seeing wild horses on the refuge, and at present the equine incursions are few and cause minimal damage. But the refuge views them as a "potential nuisance animal problem" (U.S. Fish & Wildlife Service, 2010, pp. 2–3) that will become a concern if their population increases.

Like their brethren to the south, Currituck horses that expanded their range north through Back Bay NWR and False Cape SP were getting killed on the roads of Sandbridge. Donna Snow, former Virginia Beach animal control officer and Corolla Wild Horse Fund director, formed the Virginia Wild Horse Rescue, a nonprofit charity dedicated to protecting wild horses that come into Virginia from North Carolina. Working with the Sandbridge Civic League, she organized a response team to capture and return the wild horses to Currituck County. If horses migrate into the park, the refuge, or the neighborhood of Sandbridge, the Virginia Wild Horse Rescue is pressed into action to remove them.

When horses wander through the refuge into the Sandbridge section of Virginia Beach, Virginia Horse Rescue mobilizes to capture them and return them to the safety of Currituck Banks.

The development boom continues on Currituck Banks, and a proposed bridge that will connect Corolla directly to the North Carolina mainland will encourage more visitors. The northern reaches of Currituck Banks are becoming more appealing to developers. As of 2010, there were 3,090 platted lots and more than 1,300 existing homes, including mansions with more than 20 bedrooms, in this area. The current herd management plan does not offer much hope for the future, stating that "as the northern Currituck Banks grow and develop . . . confinement, relocation or other strategies may be necessary to maintain a viable herd" (County of Currituck, 2007). One very workable solution would inevitably recruit enthusiastic support from a large contingent of taxpayers and rabid resistance from state and federal officials and others: allow the Currituck horses to expand their range into the adjoining False Cape SP and Back Bay NWR and even into nearby Mackay Island NWR, which together cover about 22,000 acres/8,900 ha—an area almost half again as large as all of Assateague Island. In fact, federal and state governments could nearly treble the range available to the

Coastal States Herds and Ranges (2014 statistics)

Herd	Population	Range (acres/ha)	Acres/ha per horse
Assateague Island			
Maryland	~100	9,761/3,950	~97.6/39.5
Virginia			
North herd	~100	2,695–3,399/	~27–34/
		1,091–1,376	~10.9–13.8
South herd	~50	547/221	~10.9/4.4
Mt. Rogers National Recreation Area/Grayson Highlands State Park (Va.)			
Mt. Rogers NRA	~100	140,000–200,000/	~1,400–2,000/
		56,656–80,937	~567–809
Grayson Highlands SP	~45	4,822/1,951	~107.2/42.4
Currituck Banks	100	7,544/3,053	63.9/25.9
Ocracoke	18	180/73	6.7/2.7
Shackleford Banks	~107	2,990/1,210	~24.9/10.1
Rachel Carson NCNERR	~30	1,073/434	~35.8/14.5
Cedar Island	~39		
Cumberland Island	~143	25,734–25,802/	~238.3–238.9/
		10,414–10,442	96.4–96.7
Western HAs & HMAs	~15,000 –31,500	~28,896,000/ 11,694,000	~917.3–1926.4/ ~371.2–779.6

Herds shrink and grow continually with or without artificial population control, and census-taking methods are diverse. Ranges also change because of management practices and natural processes. In the West, for example, federal agencies have reduced the area designated for mustangs by one third since 1971. In the East, shoreline erosion has taken valuable range from the barrier island herds. On the Virginia end of Assateague, the Chincoteague Fire Company seasonally adjusts the north herd's range. Published range figures disagree because of differences in calculation, definition, and record keeping and because of various methods of accounting for surface water, easements, and inholdings. Further, fragmented, partly developed ranges such as Currituck Banks are not exactly equivalent to contiguous, undeveloped ones such as Shackleford Banks. Despite the fog, it is clear that all the wild herds of the East Coast except the ponies of Grayson Highlands are much more crowded than Western mustangs. Some of the Eastern herds inhabit lush, well-watered environments that potentially support more animals per acre than arid Western lands. Like mustangs, most of the East Coast herds have been arbitrarily banned from government land near, sometimes within, the preserves they inhabit. The most notable example in the East is Ocracoke Island, where the Park Service owns 4,578 acres/1,853 ha, but restricts the herd to 180 acres/73 ha of fenced pasture, about 3.9% of the space available, and most of the horses spend most of their time in smaller paddocks near the barn.

wild herds of North Carolina, Virginia, and Maryland by opening almost 73 mi^2/189 km^2 near and adjoining, but mostly *within*, preserves where the herds already live. This accommodation would not be quite as simple as the stroke of a pen or the turn of a key, and it would not be free of cost; but the greatest obstacles to its realization are bureaucratic, political, and attitudinal.

Commercial development is not permitted on the north beach, but property owners and developers have been trying to change its zoning. In 2010, Swan Beach Corolla, LLC (owned by developer Gerald Friedman), asked the Currituck County Planning Board to rezone 37.36 acres/15 ha in Swan Beach, part of the 4-wheel-drive area where the wild horses live, from residential to general business. Friedman proposed an inn with up to 302 units in Swan Beach. This complex would include a wellness center, indoor and outdoor pools, a fishing pier, stores, a helipad, a chapel, a fire and rescue station, and "a corral for the wild horses" (McCalpin, 2010, March 2). Ironically, the proposed name of this environmentally destructive hotel is Swan Beach Preserve. If these land tracts are developed, the horses will be restricted to even less land, and both horses and humans are more likely to suffer injury from the resulting overly close contact. Meanwhile, development arbitrarily ruled noncommercial continues. Although motels are banned, it is legal to cover a motel-size tract with large rental cottages that accommodate comparable numbers of people.

The species most damaging to the barrier island environment is not horses, but humankind. People tramp over, drive across, and slide down dunes that are easily degraded by these activities. They leave behind plastic bags, plastic and glass bottles, and other trash. They sully ground water with sewage, vehicular fluids, and other contaminants. To protect buildings and infrastructure, they disrupt natural processes and environmental balance.

In 2001, the Corolla Wild Horse Fund incorporated as a standalone nonprofit organization. In 2006, three full-time staff members took the reins of the organization. It converted the old Corolla schoolhouse to a Wild Horse Museum that offered activities such as wooden-horse painting and discussions. In 2012, the organization moved to a larger building across the street. Children can get personal with Corolla horses when a rescued mustang comes to visit

Herd manager Wesley Stallings assesses the health of a newborn colt.

regularly during the warm season. A membership program allows concerned citizens from all over the United States to become a part of the wild-horse preservation efforts. A Web site that receives more than 1 million hits annually serves as an information hub at www.corollawildhorses.com and includes a lively, poignant blog to keep enthusiasts up to date with the herd happenings.

Wesley Stallings was the manager of the Currituck herd for many years, and the author rode with him on several occasions. Almost every day he patrolled the area north of the fence, counting horses, looking for injuries and problems, monitoring trends, and evaluating habitat. Stallings tracked the bands of horses by stallion according to their range. He carried a notebook in which he recorded the characteristics and habits of each horse, but he did not name them, tag them, or brand them. He was well acquainted with every individual in the herd. "We don't know the specifics of family lines within the herd," said Stallings (personal communication, May 25, 2010). "The main thrust is land management."

Like the current manager Christina Reynolds, Stallings worked with the Fish and Wildlife Service and the Currituck NCNERR to protect the herd over the long term while maintaining ecological balance. "It is important that the work we do now is a permanent fix," explained Stallings. "Up until now, we had been putting Band Aids on our problems" (personal communication, May 25, 2010).

The herd managers work toward implementing a geographic information system to make his data accessible to lawmakers, scientists, and others. A GIS can help people collect, store, and analyze data associated with a particular location, merging cartography, statistical analysis, and database technologies. Stallings explained "GIS can create an evidence based model that people can relate to. When legislators want to implement some system with the horses, the GIS can illustrate where the horses range and how they utilize the environment" (personal communication, May 25, 2010).

One would think managing a wild horse herd would be an idyllic career. In reality, CWHF herd managers are on call around the clock and have as little downtime as a mother with a new baby. At home, the telephone is always ringing. A common scenario occurs when a horse lies down in someone's yard to take a nap. Unfamiliar with the habits of horses, the property owner calls 911 to report a dead horse. The emergency dispatcher calls the manager, and the manager talks to the person who made the report. Often by the time the manager has arrived, the horse has awakened and wandered off.

People call when they see someone feeding a wild horse. He gets frequent calls reporting a lame horse—the horse in question has a chronically locking patella and sometimes drags her toe. Tour guides show off for tourists by calling with insignificant questions, hoping to increase their tips.

A near-wilderness in the 1980s, the beaches north of Corolla are now subject to heavy vehicular traffic. Between 2006 and 2009, wild-horse tour companies proliferated, and the number of beach drivers mushroomed. The beach and unpaved roads became deeply rutted from vehicular overuse, the beach was like a parking lot, and inexperienced off-road drivers swerved unpredictably in a nerve-wracking semblance of urban rush hour. Karen McCalpin, director of the Corolla Wild Horse Fund, says that in July, up to 3,000 vehicles a day drive up and down the beach and behind the dunes.

According to the Wild Horse Fund, one company, operator of two "monster" buses and at least one large SUV, was planning to set up a commercial riding stable among the wild herds. In June 2009 a group of riders on three domestic horses led two other horses up the beach to the tour company's property to the north. A sanctuary patrol officer stopped them and explained that even vaccinated domestic horses

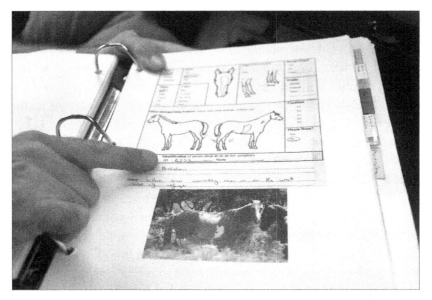

Wesley Stallings, former herd manager for the Corolla Wild Horse Fund, points out a data sheet describing the most colorful horse in the Currituck herd. This stallion has sabino coloration with a bold slash of white on his barrel. One of his sons carries a similar white marking. The rabicano gene, expressed by areas of roaning, is also present in the herd.

can carry diseases to which the wild horses have no immunity and that the wild stallions are likely to charge and injure intruders.

The riders, at least one of whom had been drinking, were defiant and continued their ride, "allowing a bikini clad woman to step from the bed of her truck into the saddle and go for a pony ride of sorts" (McCalpin, 2009, June 29). A wild stallion crossed the dune line and charged the intruders to protect his harem. One of the horses reared and threw its rider. Sheriff's deputies repeatedly chased the stallion back. The rider remounted and the group continued up the beach, chatting with beachgoers along the way. Now a county ordinance prohibits riding on the beach or keeping domestic horses anywhere in the wild horse range.

As of 2010, any agency offering tours to see the wild horses must have permits, must include a guide, and must have signs on its vehicles. The county regulation will go a long way toward reducing traffic on the beach. In an attempt to make the tours more informative and less disruptive to the lives of the horses, the Corolla Wild Horse Fund educates guides in local history, equine behavior, and procedures for safe and legal horse-watching. The organization's Web site maintains a list of approved tour agencies that are compliant with regulations.

The best way to see the horses is to accompany the herd manager on his rounds. With the purchase of a Mustang Defender membership at the $250 level, two people can ride with the manager for about 4 hr, observing and even participating in census taking, record keeping, and other daily tasks. This trip is educational and individualized, it offers excellent opportunities for photographs, and every dollar goes to help the wild horses.

The Corolla herd represents one of the rarest strains of Colonial Spanish Horses. In the absence of proper management, they will become extinct. Horse breeds are always changing, and there is always a balance to be struck between keeping bloodlines pure and losing genetic diversity. Too much diversity, and the uniqueness of the population is lost; too little, and the population will collapse, and the uniqueness of the population will still be lost.

The horse has 64 chromosomes. To conceive a foal, the stallion and mare each contribute 32 chromosomes to the new individual, which come together at conception. Only half of each parent's genes are passed along to a given foal. These genes are passed randomly. A single foal can receive only half of each parent's genes; but if each horse has many foals, chances are that most of their genes will be perpetuated in the next generation. The larger the population, the better the odds. A coin flipped 10 times may yield eight heads; but if flipped 1,000 times the occurrence of heads will approach 50%. Horse groups become genetically uniform over time when certain genes are not passed on. In a small, closed population, only new mutations can increase genetic variability.

Large populations mating freely over generations tend to form homogeneous and stable herds with many genes circulating. Rare traits often linger silently within the herd's genome, manifesting episodically. Small populations, however, tend toward homogeneity and *instability*, either emphasizing or eliminating rare genes and new mutations. Slight differences in mortality or reproductive success can have dramatic effects on the population, causing certain traits to suddenly predominate or disappear.

The location of each gene is fixed on the chromosome. Each parent contributes one gene at each location, which at conception unites

Newborn foals are becoming an uncommon sight on Currituck Banks with the implementation of the immunocontraceptive program. Colonial Spanish Horses are endangered as a breed, but the Bankers are especially rare, with only about 100 breeding mares between the Corolla and Shackleford herds.

with its counterpart to form a pair of genes at each location. The two paired genes are called alleles. When the code for both alleles is identical, they are homozygous; if each allele is different, they are heterozygous. For example, a horse homozygous for the black gene will have two copies of it. If he is heterozygous, he will have one black gene and one gene for another color at that location.

A dominant gene expresses itself if the horse has either one or two genes for the trait. For example, black is dominant over chestnut; so if either gene is for a black coat, the horse's coat will be black. A recessive gene expresses itself only if the horse has two genes for the trait. A horse will have a chestnut coat only if he is homozygous—has two genes—for chestnut. If one of those two is for black, that gene will express itself as a black coat while the chestnut gene remains unexpressed. Many traits involve multiple alleles (such as the modifying genes that cause a bay horse to express black only on the mane, tail, and legs), and some traits are incompletely dominant.

When animals in a group are less closely related, healthier dominant genes usually balance rare, disease-producing recessive ones. Recessive genes are masked by dominant alleles and can skip many generations without making their presence known. When animals breed with close relatives, recessive genes are less likely to be balanced by dominant genes, and deformities and disease become likely. Many genetic diseases result from the coupling of hidden recessive genes, including cataract blindness, dwarfism, parrot-mouth, club-foot deformities, lethal white syndrome in pinto horses, and severe combined immunodeficiency in Arabians. A shallow gene pool can also decrease reproductive ability, size, and resistance to disease.

In wild herds with limited diversity, foals with genetic problems often simply die, usually before they can reproduce. Managers of wild herds can allow nature to take its course, or can intervene by increasing genetic diversity, removing diseased horses, or sterilizing horses with undesirable genes.

Isolated herds of fewer than 200 horses tend to lose dominant alleles through inbreeding (a loss of variability that occurs when close relatives frequently mate) and though genetic drift (horses in a group happen to mate and randomly pass along some genes but not others). For example, the once-present gene that causes a solid color to turn gray/white has evidently been lost from the genome of the Corolla herd. The graying gene is dominant; so if it remained, there would be some gray horses.

The original 1997 Currituck Outer Banks Wild Horse Management Plan, signed by representatives of the Corolla Wild Horse Fund, Currituck County, Currituck NCNERR, Currituck NWR, and the Fish and Wildlife Service, allowed 60 horses to remain free-roaming on the northern Outer Banks. This number was not scientifically calculated (E.G. Cothran, personal communication, April 20, 2011), but was "merely a number upon which all parties were able to agree after prolonged and contentious debate" (Corolla Wild Horse Fund, 2008, p. 1). Cothran (personal communication, April 20, 2011) explained, "That is not a viable number, particularly for a population that has already had a great erosion of genetic variability. That population at one time was down below 20 individuals in the early 1990s."

Bhattacharyya, Slocombe, and Murphy write, "To broadly discuss all free-ranging horses in the region as though they were a homogenous group, and to generalize about their origins or management, demonstrates an oversimplified understanding of the heterogeneity of the horse populations and landscape" (2011, p. 620). Upon becoming the first executive director of the Corolla Wild Horse Fund in 2006, McCalpin immediately recognized that if the herd were managed at 60 animals, there would eventually be a complete genetic collapse similar to that experienced by the Ocracoke herd. The DNA testing performed in 1992 by Cothran collected DNA samples via dart gun to get current information about the 90-member herd's genetic health and showed that the Corolla horses have less genetic diversity than any other horse breed. He wrote that "much of the genetic diversity expected to be present in a horse population is gone, and this cannot be recovered" (2008, p. 2). Additionally, analysis of the mitochondrial DNA passed from mother to daughter showed that all the Corolla horses descend from a single maternal line.

McCalpin blamed inbreeding for a higher incidence of genetic disorders affecting the Corolla horses. A number of individuals are afflicted with locked stifles—an intermittent immobility where the hind leg joins the body. She said that if the number of horses is reduced to 60, Corolla would be seeing more horses with this problem, as well as overbites, crooked legs, and other conditions associated with inbreeding.

Conservation geneticists give the minimal sustainable effective population size as 50 individuals, and effective size should be ⅓ to ⅕ census size. (E.G. Cothran, personal communication, September 10, 2014). In other words, to be sustainable over the long term, a healthy herd should have 180–300 individuals. The number is higher for a genetically compromised group. Individually, none of the barrier islands have the forage to support herds of this size, but if the North Carolina herds are viewed as a single population, translocation of individuals between the groups can maintain genetic health.

Not all scientists agree. "The issue of what constitutes a genetically viable population has been turned into a bumper sticker issue," says reproductive physiologist Jay Kirkpatrick (personal communication, April 12, 2011). "There is no empirical evidence or data to support any of the numbers thrown around. They are theoretical and there are a lot of data to show that very low numbers are able to rebound with vigor." This seems to be the case with the sika elk of Assateague Island; the apparently robust population was founded by only seven individuals in the 1920's.

Vega-Pla, Calderón, Rodríguez-Gallardo, Martínez, and Rico (2006) studied the Retuertas horse or *Caballo de las retuertas*, a rare strain native to the Andalusia region of Spain. These horses closely resemble the horses that roamed that area in prehistoric times. Calderón noted that the present Retuertas horse population had passed though a genetic bottleneck of tens of horses and shows no sign of inbreeding depression. The team concluded that genetic variability and demographic and stochastic factors play a greater role in long-term survival than a specific numerical threshold. Likewise, the robust heard of 400-odd sika deer on Assateague Island arose from 7 animals released in 1923.

Kirkpatrick points out that the subject of minimum viable population, though important, has gotten entangled in nonscientific agendas.

> The MVP number for ASIS has been determined to be 48 and 52 for the Pryors, but these are only theoretical and have no empirical data to support them. Unless reproduction is failing, for physiological (genetic inbreeding depression) reasons, there is no genetic issue. (Personal communication, May 28, 2014)

Yet reproductive failure is a late sign of a shrinking gene pool. The herd north of Corolla, N.C., is still fecund, but genetic analysis shows genetic variability to be dangerously low. Its inbreeding expresses itself with an increase of recessive disorders, such as locking stifles that require surgical correction.

In her capacity as a certified nurse-midwife, the author serves a largely "plain" population in Lancaster County, Pennsylvania. These Amish and Mennonites descend from a small founder population, and tend to marry within their own groups. Over time they have experienced an erosion of genetic variability that reveals itself in a high rate of serious disorders, including severe combined immunodeficiency (SCID), microcephaly, many types of potentially lethal inborn errors of metabolism, and other conditions that are rare in the general population. For example, Ellis-van Creveld Syndrome, an often-lethal form of dwarfism, occurs once in about 60,000 live births in the general population. Among Old Order Amish, the rate is greater than 1 in 200 live births. Yet contraction of the gene pool has not diminished fertility. It is common for families to have 8, 12, or even more children. So far, most of them are born healthy.

When isolated herds undergo a population crash, they tend to reproduce rapidly and soon regain their former size. But each crash inevitably creates a genetic bottleneck, weakening the health of the herd and making all members more uniform. In a small, closely related population like the horses of Currituck Banks, diversity is more important than numbers alone if they are to survive for the long haul. A herd of 60 genetically diverse horses is more likely to to thwart the specter of extinction than a herd of 150 inbred animals.

In 2009, there were only about 100 breeding mares between the Shackleford and Corolla herds. This decline prompted the Equus Survival Trust, a nonprofit organization committed to protecting heirloom equine breeds, to change the status of the Banker Colonial Spanish Mustang to Critical/Nearly Extinct.

The population of Corolla horses bloomed well beyond the 60-horse legal maximum. The census-takers counted 119 horses in 2006, 94 in 2007, 101 in 2008, 88 in 2009, 115 in 2010. Forty-two horses were removed from Currituck Banks between 2006 and 2008, and 33 of these were placed in adoptive homes. The census of 2011 counted 121 horses. In that year, 16 foals were born, and Stallings contracepted 53 mares with the immunocontraceptive porcine zona pellucida (PZP).

In 2014, at about the time this book went to press, the population was 100 horses, and McCalpin had administered contraceptive vaccines to all the mares with the help of retired police officer E.T. Smith. Only 2 foals were born in 2014. One, a spunky colt named Vivo, was removed from the wild with his mother for the correction of congenitally contracted tendons which forced him to walk on the tips of his hooves. Only one 2014 foal remains in the wild, a leggy filly named Primavera.

The National Academy of Science, in its 2013 report on the genetic health of Western herds, recommended that the smaller populations should be regarded as a single herd, and managers should exchange horses between groups to maintain genetic diversity:

> The committee recommends routine [genetic] monitoring at
> all gathers and the collection and analysis of a sufficient

number of samples to detect losses of diversity. The committee also recommends that BLM consider at least some animals on different HMAs as a single population and use the principles of metapopulation theory to direct management activities that attain and maintain the level of genetic diversity needed for continued survival, reproduction, and adaptation to changing environmental conditions. . . . Although there is no minimum viable population size above which a population can be considered forever viable, studies suggest that thousands of animals will be needed for long-term viability and maintenance of genetic diversity. Few HMAs are large enough to buffer the effects of genetic drift and herd sizes must be maintained at prescribed AMLs, so managing HMAs as a metapopulation will reduce the rate of reduction of genetic diversity over the long term. (National Research Council, 2013, p. 9)

In July 2014, McCalpin and Cothran collected DNA samples from horses in the Cedar Island, N.C., herd via dart gun to evaluate possible candidates for genetic exchange. Although there have been horses on Cedar Island for more than 100 years, many in the current population were translocated from Shackleford Banks after most of the original herd was euthanized for carrying equine infectious anemia. Both the Corolla and Shackleford/Cedar herds appear to have descended from the same original population, and mating between the two groups would not be considered crossbreeding. Shackleford Banks horses, however, are genetically healthy, with three maternal lines where Corolla has only one.

A sound stallion, given the opportunity, can impregnate many mares simultaneously and shift the herd genome toward better health more rapidly than a mare, which almost never carries more than one foal at a time. But for stallions, reproductive success is far from certain. Before he gets a chance to breed, a mature male must fight seasoned stallions to win mares and retain them in his harem. Many young stallions do not have the skills to entice mares and fight or bluff to keep them. If the Corolla Wild Horse Fund introduces an outside stallion who is unable to assemble a harem, he will have no genetic impact. And artificial insemination is not an option, as on a panicky wild mare, the procedure would require capture and anesthesia.

Though most Corolla wild horses appear healthy and robust, inbreeding has caused a high rate of genetic defects in the herd. The Corolla Wild Horse Fund increased gene flow by adding a young stallion from the Cedar Island herd, and plans to introduce mares from compatible, genetically diverse populations.

Cothran analyzed the DNA of the two most promising prospects, then rejected a gorgeous silver dapple colt because he carried the gene for multiple congenital ocular anomalies. Ultimately, on November 20, 2014, the Corolla Wild Horse Fund introduced a stallion from the Cedar Island herd. The veterinarian found him healthy, and analysis of his DNA proved that he is a Colonial Spanish horse without identified genetic disease. Named for Gus Cothran, who was instrumental in this revitalization project, the stallion will breathe new life into a dying gene pool if he successfully mates with Corolla mares. The Corolla Wild Horse Fund hopes to introduce Cedar Island mares in the future. Cedar Island horses, most of which carry Shackleford Banks bloodlines, are genetically similar to the Corollas and will keep the breed pure, but are different enough to add new alleles.

Low genetic diversity and low numbers are the two greatest hreats to the Corolla herd. When the census is very low, the herd is vulnerable to destruction by disease, drought, fire, flood, or hurricane. This risk is very real. On Cumberland Island NS, a 1990 outbreak of mosquito-borne Eastern equine encephalitis killed about 40 horses.

On Assateague Island, at least 15 horses died of EEE in a 5-year span, and 12 drowned in a single storm.

The critically endangered Colonial Spanish Horses on Great Abaco Island in the Bahamas numbered an estimated 200 in the mid-20th century, but, excluded from habitat, gunned down for sport and from antipathy, and attacked by dogs, dwindled to a low of three individuals in the 1970s. Wild horse advocates intervened to save the remaining animals, and by 1992, the herd had increased to 35. But when Hurricane Floyd struck in 1999, storm damage and resulting fires pushed the horses onto a citrus plantation. The rich forage on the plantation caused obesity, decreased fertility, and crippling laminitis, and herbicides, pesticides, and poisonous plants caused extensive liver damage. As of this writing, the once-thriving herd has been reduced to a single aging mare named Nunki. According to Milanne Rehor of the Wild Horses of Abaco Preservation Society, reproductive specialists are attempting to harvest ova from Nunki, in hopes of fertilizing them with sperm from genetically appropriate stallions and gestating them in surrogate mares (personal communication, February 17, 2014).

In the Dzungarian Gobi of southwest Mongolia, a critically endangered population of Przewalski horses was thriving and rapidly increasing its numbers until a harsh, stormy winter devastated it. Frequent blizzards and subzero cold reduced the Przewalski population from 137 horses in December 2009 to 48 in April 2010. Whereas the herd typically increased by 28–36 foals annually, a solitary foal was born in 2010. It will take many years for the herd to reach its projected minimum viable population of 200–300, and another disaster could easily wipe it out entirely. Even at the minimum size for genetic sustainability, the herd will remain vulnerable to natural disaster. The world population of the species, including zoo stock, is only about 1,400 animals.

Over the long term, the Corolla herd is likely to experience genetic collapse and extinction within a few generations if managed at 60 animals. As Sponenberg wrote to McCalpin in 2008,

> In this, as in other cases, the competing interests need to somehow come to an effective compromise. I don't know what that will look like, but I do know that if a genetically isolated horse population is to be genetically secure for the

A mare crosses a tangle of sand fencing in the village of Carova. The sure-footedness of Banker horses is legendary, largely because they learn to negotiate endlessly varied obstacles in their life in the wild.

> future, then the total population must be much closer to 100 than 60. (*H.R. 306, Corolla Wild Horses Protection Act*, 2011b)

The Corolla population's best chance for survival lies in increasing its numbers and introducing outside horses occasionally to maintain genetic diversity over the long term. To that end, U.S. Representative Walter B. Jones (NC 3) introduced the Corolla Wild Horses Protection Act (H.R. 5482) to the 111th Congress on June 8, 2010. This legislation was to establish a partnership between the secretary of the Interior and the Corolla Wild Horse Fund similar to that between the Park Service and the Foundation for Shackleford Horses, which allows for a target population of 120–130 horses and occasional introductions of horses from Shackleford Banks. After it died in committee, Jones introduced a new bill (H.R. 306) with the same title to the 112th Congress on January 18, 2011. It was approved by the House Natural Resources Committee on October 5, 2011, despite a written dissent by six members from northern and western states (H.R. Rep. No. 112-210, 2011), and was unanimously passed by the House on February 6, 2012. It died there when the 112th Congress went home. On January

If enough people work together to protect them, wild horses will continue to roam free on the Outer Banks.

3, 2013, the first day of the 113th Congress, Jones reintroduced the bill once more as H.R. 126. It once again passed the House unanimously on June 3, 2013, and is now waiting to pass the Senate, with chance of being enacted that one source estimates at 20% .

Passage of this bill would allow horses to roam anywhere on the refuge unless credible scientific evidence shows that they threaten survival of an endangered species for which the refuge is critical habitat. The bill is supported by the Wild Horse Fund, former North Carolina Governor Beverly Perdue, Marc Basnight (former president *pro tempore* of the North Carolina State Senate), the Humane Society of the United States, the County of Currituck, the Animal Welfare Institute, the Foundation for Shackleford Horses, Saving America's Mustangs, American Wild Horse Preservation Campaign, and Equus Survival Trust.

But a healthy herd of sustainable size would raise anew the old question, "Where will these horses live?" Detractors maintain that the purpose of the refuge is to support what they consider wild-life, including waterfowl, migratory birds, and endangered species. McCalpin pointed out that at Shackleford Banks on Cape Lookout NS, the National Park Service maintains 120–130 horses on a 3,000-acre/1,200-ha range. Over the past 12 years, there has been no documented negative impact to the seashore. Yet the comparable number of Corolla horses stand accused of damaging the 7,544 acres/3,053 ha where they roam, most of it private land.

The Fish and Wildlife Service opposes this bill, as do The Wildlife Society, the National Wildlife Refuge Association, Defenders of Wildlife, Ducks Unlimited, the Public Lands Foundation, and the North Carolina Wildlife Federation. To the National Wildlife Refuge Association, the leading nonprofit support group for the refuge system, wild horses are as unwelcome as feral cats or hogs. Its Web site opines,

> Like the kudzu vine that ravages southeastern states, or the Burmese python in Florida, feral horses are an introduced species that can wreak havoc on native plants and wildlife. . . .
>
> The so-called "Corolla Wild Horses" that roam the Outer Banks venture onto Currituck National Wildlife Refuge and trample a fragile ecosystem that many native species depend on. (Woolford, 2012)

The declaration is at odds with the fact that the horses were resident for hundreds of years before the refuge was established, including during the 19th century, when waterfowl populations were at their zenith. Although the Association does not necessarily speak for the Fish and Wildlife Service, the agency seems to have made no effort to distance itself from this inflammatory statement.

The Congressional Budget Office calculated that managing the horses on the refuge would cost $200,000 a year. The nonprofit Corolla Wild Horse Fund would absorb all costs of horse management, including census-taking, record keeping, health inspection, removal of animals unfit for the wild, and population control. The Fish and Wildlife Service has expressed doubt that the refuge can support additional horses without compromising the environment, and it asserts that the bill is at odds with the refuge's mission. The Corolla Wild Horse Fund says, however, that if the bill were signed into law, the Fish and Wildlife Service's role in horse management would not change. Because the Currituck Refuge is a satellite of Mackay Island NWR with no permanently assigned staff, it appears the only active role the agency has taken in horse management has been pressing to have the horses thinned or removed.

While today the Fish and Wildlife Service considers horses "exotic and potentially damaging to vegetation under active management," in the 1940s the agency thought otherwise. Rachel Carson, internationally celebrated marine biologist, environmentalist, and editor-in-chief for the Fish and Wildlife Service, observed that the presence of 300 head of cattle and horses grazing the Chincoteague NWR was "not detrimental to the waterfowl for which the refuge was established" (1947, p. 17).

Michael Hutchins, former Executive Director and CEO of The Wildlife Society, maintains that feral horses trample soils and vegetation, change the distribution and abundance of native plant species and nutrients, selectively consume palatable plants, and disturb avian nesting sites. He testified at a hearing in April 2011 the legislation would make it more difficult for the Fish and Wildlife Service to manage the feral horses on Currituck NWR and hamper the refuge system's mission. It would put the Fish and Wildlife Service in the difficult position of being legislatively required to manage for the conservation of native wildlife and habitat on the one hand and to support what it deems a non-native invasive species on the other.

Do wild horses cause permanent environmental damage to their home ranges? Research has shown that they do—and that they do not. Promoters and detractors alike can draw on a large body of evidence to support their positions. Taken as a whole, these studies appear to demonstrate that in the absence of overpopulation, horses and other grazers harmonize with and even benefit the rest of the natural world, and species disrupted by their activities typically rebound quickly from damage.

Numerous studies have documented or suggested detrimental or potentially harmful effects of free-roaming herbivores. Nimmo and Miller (2007, p. 409) compiled a list of adverse environmental effects of wild horses, which the author has adapted:

- Soil loss, compaction, and erosion
- Trampling of vegetation
- Reduced plant diversity
- Killing native trees by chewing bark
- Damage to bog habitat
- Damage to water bodies
- Facilitated weed invasion
- Altered community composition and reproductive habitat of birds, fish, crabs, small mammals, reptiles, and ants

- Fewer birds
- Reduced plant biomass and salt marsh vegetation
- Lower diversity and density of fishes

Conversely, many researchers have demonstrated the beneficial or potentially beneficial effects of the grazing of large herbivores on ecosystems, especially wetlands and grasslands. Documented beneficial environmental effects of feral horses include

- Dispersing seeds of desirable native plants
- Benefiting endangered reptiles
- Promoting biological diversity, accelerating succession, and encouraging a diverse mosaic of desirable plants
- Increasing nutritional value of forage
- Increasing browse vital to winter survival of deer and elk
- Providing feeding, nesting, dusting, and display sites for upland and passerine birds
- Breaking up homogeneous grass stands, producing a patchy, open cover with a diversity of forbs
- Enhancing regrowth of forbs beneficial to wildfowl
- Greatly increasing diversity of bird species
- Altering community composition of birds, increasing foraging habitat for willets, least sandpipers and other birds that prey on small invertebrates
- Greatly reducing height and density of invasive *Phragmites*

Horses beneficially remove excess vegetation from the most productive plant communities and break up dense, tall stands of *Phragmites australis*, the common reed, giving desirable plants a competitive advantage. *Phragmites* has been present in North America for tens of thousands of years and is considered a native species in both inland and coastal areas. Pieces of native *Phragmites* were found in the fossilized dung of a Shasta ground sloth dating to 40,000 years ago.

Over the past two centuries, an introduced strain, likely from Europe or Asia, has overtaken wetlands throughout the United States. When developers removed woody vegetation bordering the marshes from Maine southward and ditched tidal wetlands for mosquito control, nitrogen-rich freshwater runoff inundated coastal marshes, lowering salinity and giving *Phragmites* a competitive edge. About 90% of the *Phragmites* dominance is attributable to shoreline development. When nitrogen is abundant, tall plants such as

Numerous studies have shown that balanced grazing by horses in salt marshes actually improves the habitat for many species of waterfowl.

Phragmites capture much of the available sunlight and squeeze out their shorter rivals, sharply decreasing the diversity of marsh vegetation and decreasing productivity of fish and shellfish. Once *Phragmites* has taken hold, it is difficult and expensive to subdue.

The invasive reed is nutritious and palatable to horses, and grazing pressures weaken its unwanted foothold on estuarine margins. When horses bite off *Phragmites* shoots below water level, the plant often starts to decompose and may die. Under heavy grazing, *Phragmites* declines quickly in height and density, allowing sunlight to reach competing native plants. *Phragmites* grows tall and dense in ungrazed exclosures, but it is low and sparse in heavily grazed areas. In France, Duncan and D'Herbes (1982) found that by breaking up *Phragmites* stands, horses increase the area of open water and the abundance of submerged plants.

Refuge officials maintain that horses spread the seeds of non-native plants through their manure; this accusation is true. Free-roaming horses live most of their lives in well-defined home ranges and eat problem vegetation such as *Phragmites* with desirable species such as *Spartina*. In one study, non-native species did sprout in dung piles, but then so did native species, which were often at a competitive advantage. The study concluded that since horses avoid grazing where they have defecated, these dung piles might represent "refuges for palatable species," including natives, to take hold (Loydi & Zalba, 2009, p. 107).

Of course, horses can only spread the seeds of plants that exist within their range. In 1985, Davison found exotic plant species had become established in the Ocracoke pony pen, such as Bermuda grass (*Cynodon dactylon*), annual buttercup (*Ranunculus sardous*), and some pasture grasses, introduced when the Park Service fed hay in winter. The author concluded that these exotic plant species did not endanger the native plants beyond the enclosure. Seeds are spread by other herbivores as well and by wind and water. Wild birds are more numerous than horses, travel much farther, and distribute many more seeds in their droppings.

Horses do alter the environmental balance of the salt marsh, but not necessarily to its detriment. On Shackleford Banks, horse grazing changes the marshes from nesting habitat for gulls and terns to a bountiful feeding ground used by a diverse community of foraging shorebirds. Willets and least sandpipers *prefer* grazed marshes and are nearly absent from ungrazed marshes. Marshes used by ungulates support large populations of crabs, which in turn attract birds that feed on them. Although the number of individual birds is greater in marshes that were not grazed by horses, grazed marshes show much greater diversity. One study showed that twice as many avian species foraged in the marshlands used by horses—20 species versus 10 (Levin et al., 2002). Likewise, Zalba and Cozzani (2004) examined the impact of wild horses on bird communities in the Pampas tall grasslands in Argentina. They found that diversity and total abundance of birds were greatest with moderate grazing, decreased in ungrazed areas, and greatly decreased under high grazing pressure although some species preferred intensely grazed areas.

Disturbance by large herbivores *increases* the diversity and quality of wildlife habitat, creating a patchwork of food resources. Research has demonstrated that light to moderate grazing does damage plants and disrupt other wildlife, but this damage is temporary. Wood, Mengak, and Murphy (1987) studied the effects of horse grazing alongside goats, cattle, and sheep on Shackleford Banks and observed evidence of damage by these species, but expected the resilient island to recover and reestablish *Spartina* in denuded areas.

Rheinhardt and Rheinhardt found that horses on the Currituck Banks "consume few forb [herbaceous plant] species and graminoid [grass] species seem to recover from grazing by early summer when primary production is highest. . . . Because rooting impacts of feral hogs may be more severe than horse grazing impacts on Currituck Banks, exclosure experiments would have to be designed to separate horse grazing from hog rooting" (2004, p. 258).

The Currituck NWR is concerned that grazing may threaten certain endangered plants: "The effect horses have on sea beach amaranth (if any) needs to be determined, as does interdune grasslands and marshes [*sic*]" (p. 194, USFWS, 2008).

Seabeach amaranth (*Amaranthus pumilus*) is a rare plant that grows on Atlantic coastal overwash flats and on beaches above mean high tide. To thrive, this species appears to need large areas of naturally functioning barrier island beaches and inlets, and when people develop shorelines to prevent overwash, its habitat shrinks. Seabeach amaranth virtually disappeared from Cape Hatteras north after construction of the artificial dune barrier in the 1930s, and at Cape Lookout it is not found in areas used by off-road vehicles. Its numbers fluctuate dramatically from year to year in response to environmental conditions, thriving when overwash and severe storms bring seeds to the surface to germinate.

Plant counts vary widely from year to year and bear no relationship to the presence or absence of horses. On ungrazed Hatteras Point, Hatteras Inlet, and North Ocracoke, researchers counted 15,828 seabeach amaranth plants in 1988, only one in 1995, and 34 in 2003. On Cape Lookout National Seashore in 2003, the Park Service counted 206 plants on ungrazed Core Banks and 1,354 plants on the grazed Shackleford Banks—but the following year the census was 137 plants total through all of Cape Lookout NS. Interestingly, in 1995, when the herd was at its peak size of 184 horses (the Park Service had overestimated by 30% and put the population at 240), the seabeach amaranth count on Shackleford Banks was a bountiful 1,155 plants.

The Fish and Wildlife Service blames grazing animals for "reduction of vegetation, encouraging the formation of sand sheets and sand hills, destabilizing much of Currituck Banks" (U.S. Department of Interior, 2010, p. 18) and points to H.F. Hennigar, Jr's, master's thesis (1979) for corroboration. More recently, Havholm et al. (2004) used ground-penetrating radar, modern dating techniques, and soil analysis to study dune activity and stabilization along the North Carolina-Virginia coast. The team noted that "overgrazing has not had significant impact" on dune dynamics (2004, p. 993). As in other locations, dunes form where there is an adequate supply of sand on the shoreface, winds are strong enough to mobilize the sand, and there is enough moisture to support vegetation that can stabilize it. The presence of grazers does not alter this ancient process.

Plassmann et al. (2010) found that dune vegetation is influenced primarily by rainfall, and large herbivores had minimal effect on compaction and moisture retention. They also noted that vegetation appeared to benefit more from year-'round grazing than from seasonal grazing. Additionally, physical disturbance of large sand flats by horses helps to provide nesting habitat for least terns, piping plovers, and other shorebirds by delaying their colonization by perennial grasses and shrubs.

Barrier islands maintain dynamic stability by rolling over themselves toward the mainland. They can adapt to violent storm surges and sea level rise, but are weakened by cumulative stresses introduced by people, such as shore protection.

Clearly, the problem species is humans, not horses. Residential development not only changes the appearance of the landscape, it also interferes with the natural function of the barrier island system. Developers bulldoze roads, flatten home sites, and replace natural dune-building vegetation with lawns. Buildings block the flow of sand-laden wind and cause it to eddy, altering the growth and migration of dunes. Anthropogenic modifications—roads, buildings, dune ridges, planted vegetation, artificial inlet closures, and inlet stabilization disrupt natural processes that maintain the islands (Smith et al., 2008). Even the marsh impoundments constructed on federal refuges to provide habitat for waterfowl and other wildlife disrupt the natural marsh-building process and may hinder the normal migration of salt marshes in the face of rising sea levels.

The undeveloped northern part of Pea Island grew wider between 1852 and 1998 at a rate that did not change when livestock were

Horses preferentially graze *spartina* and other grasses, clipping it quite short, then moving to another area. When the equine population is in balance with its habitat, grasses have the opportunity to regrow when the band moves on to the next meadow. When the number of horses exceeds that which the environment can support, grasslands contract and horses become lean.

removed in 1935. The southern part, along with the entire Avon-Buxton area, eroded steadily over the same period. Smith et al. (2008) concluded, "Attempts to protect the barrier islands through construction and maintenance of artificial barrier dune ridges and through rapid closure of inlets (e.g., Buxton Inlet in 1963 and Isabel Inlet in 2003) promote the opposite result" (p. 80).

The dunes north of Corolla were built by nature, up to 35 ft/11 m in height, and they are riddled with overwash passes. Horses lived in and around these dunes for centuries at a much greater population density than they have now. Despite the grazing pressures from a multitude of horses, sheep, goats, cattle, and hogs, the dunes grew high and maintained their natural ever-changing equilibrium with waves and wind as they migrated westward.

In the absence of large-scale human manipulation of the environment, horses become part of this balance. Sometimes the balance results in overwash flats and island migration, opening up habitat for birds such as the piping plover. Sometimes the balance results in high dunes as in Corolla and at the west end of Shackleford Banks. Both are natural processes. If horses were invariably detrimental to dunes, mature dune systems would not have developed in Corolla and Shackleford Banks, where horses have roamed for centuries.

Detractors argue that long-domesticated horses introduced from Europe did not co-evolve with the estuarine ecosystem of the New World, and as exotics they do not belong on federal lands at all. Many wildlife scientists, however, consider the horse a reintroduced native. Although most domestic animals are subspecies of ancestral animals, *Equus caballus* remains genetically identical to its Pleistocene progenitors. Thousands of years of selective breeding have wrought changes in horses that are no more radical than those caused naturally by genetic drift.

Recently, DNA molecules were recovered from core samples of Alaskan permafrost, showing that woolly mammoths and horses persisted in interior Alaska until 7,600 years ago—or less. They may have lasted longer in locations distant from the Bering land bridge, where no permafrost, and hence no buried DNA record, exists. The horse coevolved with North American ecosystems for more than 50 million years, lived here as *E. caballus* for 3 million years, and then was absent for fewer than 8,000 years.

Pleistocene horses grazed the North American marshes into an ecological balance very similar to that produced by modern free-roaming horses. *Spartina alterniflora* evolved under the teeth of grazers, not only horses, but also proboscidians (relatives of modern elephants) and camelids (relatives of camels and llamas). So did native *Phragmites,* which evolved as a harmonious component of the primordial world. It would appear that grazing herbivores are necessary to re-create a truly natural state.

The continent was teeming with horses when the non-native Paleo-Indians expanded into the Americas. There was an abundance of other horses besides *E. caballus*, so similar in form that paleontologists distinguish the various species mainly by pattern variations of the grinding surfaces of the cheek teeth.

At the peak of the North American glaciation about 18,000 years ago, nearly 5 million mi^2/12.9 million km^2 of the earth was covered

Grass is the preferred forage for horses, but they will round out their diets with herbaceous plants, legumes, poison ivy, greenbriar, spanish moss, seaweed, twigs, and even bark from trees.

by an ice sheet 2 mi/3.2 km thick. Ocean levels were about 400 ft/122 m lower than they are at present, and what is now submerged continental shelf was exposed as much as 60–90 mi/97–145 km east of the present shoreline. The climate of the area that would someday become North Carolina was arid-cool during the height of the Ice Age, arid-hot 7,500–5,000 years ago, and thereafter warm-humid. This flat coastal plain contained bogs and swamps interspersed with scrublands of pine and deciduous species. Megafauna grazed plentifully in an open, park-like landscape of arid scrub, prairie, and savanna that probably looked much like modern-day Wyoming, rather than the dense, humid closed-canopy woodlands encountered by Europeans in the 1500s.

Human cultures made extensive changes to the environment, ecosystem functions, and evolution. Paleo-Indians intentionally burned native vegetation to drive prey, to create a favorable habitat for game species, and later to clear land for agriculture. The modern dominance of oaks, hickories, and pines in the Southeast reflects more than 12,000 years of regular burning by human inhabitants. Many scientists believe that early North American tribes contributed to the extinction of Pleistocene megafauna through overhunting.

Not long after the arrival of people, horses disappeared, and it is quite possible that Paleo-Indians helped to eradicate them. After 15,000–20,000 years of continuous residency, American Indians were naturalized as "native people." Non-native Europeans then arrived, repatriating the native wild horse and partially restoring the balance that was lost when most large ungulates died out. "Horses, like cattle, can serve as convenient proxies for the set of large mammals that inhabited the Americas during and before the Pleistocene. Horses, in fact, are more than proxies: they *are* Pleistocene megafauna" (Barlow, 2000, p. 32). A few scholars have gone so far as to suggest "Pleistocene rewilding," or attempting to re-create the ecological balance that existed before people arrived, using extant species, including wild elephants for mammoths (Donlan et al., 2006). Others doubt that we can restore the continent's virginity. Pleistocene rewilding might jeopardize existing native species and long-standing ecosystems without reestablishing the ancient balance, and it would inevitably clash with roads, fences, buildings, and people.

At a hearing for H.R. 306, Hutchins testified, "It's all about values. Do we want to protect our native wildlife, or turn our national refuges into theme parks for exotic animals?" (*H.R. 306, Corolla Wild Horses Protection Act*, 2011a). McCalpin (2011, April 13) replied, "We asked for wild horses—not elephants! . . . These horses were on this land long before we were and certainly long before USFWS purchased it."

Public land managers are reluctant to encourage horse grazing because of biases held by many professional wildlife biologists and wildlife interest groups. Clearly, overgrazing is detrimental to the environment, but the absence of large herbivores may be harmful in ways that we cannot yet comprehend. When the herd is maintained at a healthy population level, environmental harm is usually temporary, and compromised species recover quickly. As elsewhere, these free-roaming horses have acquired a bad reputation that they do not deserve.

Free-roaming horses, like any other species, change the environment with their presence. Innumerable species write in the diary of the wetlands. On any given day, broken stems mark where a band of

The wild horse herd on Cumberland Island is unmanaged, and the equine census had apparently stabilized at the carrying capacity of the island many years prior to this 2011 photograph. The population could no longer grow because mortality balanced birth rate, and the horse count was roughly the same from year to year. When years of drought reduced the available forage, many of the lactating mares on Cumberland Island had Henneke scores of 1.5–2.5, though the author noted some individuals scoring as high as 3. Muscle wasting was evident on the gaunt mares. Where horses grazed in lawn areas, grasses were continuously cropped short with bare patches, while marsh areas showed varying degrees of impact.

horses dined on *Spartina* or *Phragmites.* Impressions in the mud and a scattering of feathers announce that a hawk put an end to a songbird on a meadow's rim. Vegetation is compressed in a thicket where a deer bedded down for the day. Irregularly mounded litterfall marks where a sounder of feral hogs rooted in the forest floor. Every goose, raccoon, muskrat, duck, plover, bat, beetle, and so on down to the tiniest single microbe affects the environment by living its life as part of the web.

The magnitude of horse impact depends on many factors—population density, growth and composition, type of habitat, climatic variation, animal behavior, anthropogenic influences, and other disturbances such as fire and flood. Mitchell, Gabrey, Marra, and Erwin (2006) found that light to moderate grazing probably has little effect, but with more intense grazing, impacts accumulate.

No definition of *overgrazing* is universally accepted. Range managers, forest managers, ecologists, wildlife biologists, conservationists, politicians, journalists, and private citizens have different definitions based on their attitudes, habits, and agendas, so they cannot always agree on whether or not an area is overgrazed. Wilson and Macleod (1991, p. 481) suggest overgrazing is relatively uncommon. "Although there are some notable exceptions, there are reasonable grounds to suspect that many rangelands are not overgrazed to the extent that is frequently claimed."

Mysterud (2006) argues that the term *overgrazing* is often invoked to support management agendas:

The term 'overgrazing' (including related processes such as ... browsing and trampling) is much used and abused in scientific literature ... and it is usually value-laden as it implies grazing at a higher level than wanted relative to a specific management objective. ... it has been used to describe almost any kind of ... negative impact of grazing. Few use an explicit definition of overgrazing related to a specific ecological pattern or process. (p. 130)

Indications of overgrazing include loss of the original vegetation coverage to where recovery is progressively slower or irreversible, increasing areas of bare ground, local extinction of seed sources, and fundamental changes to successional pathways (Mysterud, 2006). But it is possible to make too much of such signs:

In virtually any grazing system, spots of bare ground can be found around water holes, salt licks, and along fences ... that may be attributed to trampling or might be considered evidence of overgrazing, even though they have no serious effect on the system. Overgrazing is an almost meaningless concept unless the spatial scale is considered. (Mysterud, p. 135)

Using Eberhardt's model (2002), as the herd reaches the carrying capacity of its habitat, sequential changes will occur in the population. First, foal mortality increases. Next, young mares produce their first foals at increasingly older ages. Third, reproductive rates decline. Finally, in extreme cases, adult mortality increases. As food

On Currituck Banks, lactating mares typically have Henneke scores of 5–6, and the herd appears in balance with its environment. This photograph was taken in May 2012. Research indicates that the effects of grazing are temporary, and grasses recover from grazing by early summer.

resources become scarce, equine bodily condition and fat reserves decline, particularly for adult mares, which require more calories than stallions to gestate and nurse foals (which they often do simultaneously). Scorolli noted that when food supplies are limited, a higher percentage of mares will show poor body condition. After a two-year study of an Argentine herd, Scorolli (2012, p. 92) concluded, "Adult males, stallions, were in good condition . . . and had higher values than adult females in all months of both years." It should follow that if the majority of lactating mares in a herd are well-fleshed, the rest of the herd is at least equally healthy, forage is abundant, and adverse environmental effects are negligible.

The body condition of lactating mares is a sensitive, easily observed, and easily quantified indicator of the health of a herd and its habitat. When food is abundant, lactating mares have more body fat, which can be assessed from a distance using the Henneke scale. As the herd approaches carrying capacity, competition for food increases, and horses lose body fat and become more vulnerable to diseases and parasites. Lactating mares require more calories than the other horses

Lactational Condition Index

LCI 1

Majority of lactating mares with Henneke scores of 1–2.

Herd less likely to survive short-term insults (for example disease, drought, harsh climatic events).

Lower mare fertility and poorer pregnancy outcomes. Pregnant and lactating mares, juveniles, and elderly horses risk higher mortality.

Range at high risk for overgrazing.

LCI 2

Majority of lactating mares with Henneke scores of 3–4.

Herd more likely to survive short-term stresses.

Higher fertility, better pregnancy outcomes, greater survival.

Range at overall lower risk for overgrazing, but may show signs of overgrazing in places favored by horses.

LCI 3

Majority of lactating mares with Henneke scores of 5–6.

Herd most likely to survive short-term stresses.

Best pregnancy outcomes, high fertility, best survival.

Range at low risk for overgrazing.

LCI 4

Majority of lactating mares with Henneke scores greater than 7.

Herd most likely to survive short-term stresses.

Best pregnancy outcomes, highest fertility, best survival. Horses with very high Henneke scores are at risk for obesity-related health problems.

Range at lowest risk for overgrazing.

If lactating mares, the horses under the greatest nutritional stress, remain in good condition, one can reliably expect to find the rest of the herd and the herd's environment in good condition. A low Lactational Condition Index at the end of the growing season is a telling indicator of individual and herd health. Lactational Index tool © Bonnie Gruenberg 2013, may be used freely with attribution.

in the herd and are the first to lose condition when food becomes scarce. If the majority of lactating mares in the herd are significantly underweight, it is likely that the food supply is insufficient to support a population of that size. This would be true whether the decline in plant production is the result of overgrazing or some other process such as development, storm damage, or drought.

At Mount Rogers National Recreation Area and the adjacent Grayson Highlands State Park, the U.S. Forest Service and the state of Virginia use Shetland Ponies to maintain scenic grassy vistas by limiting the growth of brushy plants.

While researching this book, the author made informal visual surveys of the condition of barrier island herds and observed a relationship between Henneke body condition scores of nursing mares and the health of herds as a whole and their environment. She proposes using the Lactational Condition Index described in the accompanying table to assess the health of herds and their proximity to the carrying capacity of their ranges.

An LCI score of 1 indicates that the majority of lactating mares have Henneke scores of 1–2. Their poor condition suggests that the herd is probably at or near carrying capacity, reproductively compromised, and at risk of high mortality due to malnutrition, parasites, and disease. Herds in which the majority of lactating mares have Henneke scores of 3–4 receive an LCI score of 2. These herds are generally healthier, more fecund, and have lower mortality than those with an LCI score of 1. Their ranges are at lower risk of depletion than at LCI-1, though some areas may be overused. Herds in which most lactating mares have Henneke scores greater than 5 receive LCI scores of 3 and 4. These well-nourished herds are generally healthier and optimally fecund, and their ranges are at low risk of grazing stress. Overweight mares are the most fertile, but may develop obesity-related health problems.

Disease can cause decline in condition, but disease generally involves individuals, while insufficient food production affects all lactating mares. Likewise, intestinal parasites can cause an individual's condition to decline markedly, but widespread heavy parasitic infestation tends to accompany overpopulation.

While equine overpopulation is undeniably damaging to any ecosystem, small bands that graze lightly and move on can be surprisingly beneficial. Elsewhere, land managers recognize the potential benefits of grazing. Horse grazing in the Camargue of France has proved a useful instrument for management of marshes for waterfowl by opening up the emergent vegetation, especially where the water level is controlled by the manager. Conservation groups in northern Europe have encouraged grazing in wetlands to improve habitat for ducks, coots, wigeon, and other waterfowl. Wylie (2012) found that non-native herbaceous cover increased at the expense of native herb cover on San Clemente Island grassland sites after feral herbivores were removed.

In the 1960s, the scenic balds of the Mount Rogers National Recreation Area and the adjacent Grayson Highlands State Park were becoming choked with brushy overgrowth, and fir and hardwood seedlings threatened to someday obstruct the scenic vistas. The U.S. Forest Service introduced first sheep and then cattle to feed on the brush, but they died after eating toxic plants. In 1974, the Forest Service invited Bill Pugh of Sugar Grove, Va., to graze his herd of 50+ Shetland Ponies on the mountain peaks. These ponies have successfully performed this function for nearly 40 years and are now managed by the Wilburn Ridge Pony Association. On the other hand, it can be argued that the scenic balds are not natural features, and the Mount Rogers ponies are helping to conserve an engineered environment. The herd currently numbers roughly 150 animals. The Association gathers ponies each September and sells foals at auction. Proceeds fund veterinary care for the herd and support the Rugby Volunteer Rescue Squad and Fire Department.

The Fish and Wildlife Service uses carefully managed grazing rotations as a tool to maintain healthy habitat for Attwater's prairie

Lush grass and healthy lactating mares indicate that the Currituck horses remain in balance with their habitat.

chickens. Roughly 1 million of these birds populated the Texas and Louisiana Gulf coastal prairie at the time of first European contact, their odd booming mating calls resonating over the endless grasslands each spring. The prairie chicken evolved alongside the vast herds of bison, horses, and other large herbivores that ruled the primordial tall-grass prairie. When the large grazers vanished, so did the birds. Overgrazing by cattle compounded the problem. By the 1930s, the species had dwindled to about 1% of its former population. Today, rotational grazing has helped to reestablish the bird in its native ranges.

Historically, land managers have tried to preserve natural communities by protecting them from physical disturbance. They have come to understand that many forms of disturbance benefit the environment and maintain the natural balance.

The Fish and Wildlife Service may grant ponies a role in the management of impoundments on the Chincoteague NWR. Currently the staff uses disturbances such as burning, discing with a tractor, and mowing to enhance the habitat for migrating birds. Lou Hinds, former refuge manager, said,

> We are considering . . . moving some portion of the herd into one of the impoundments to allow the ponies to graze on the plants for a while, to clear away undergrowth and use their hooves to punch in seed. The waste will be broken down by

other invertebrates and microorganisms, and that becomes nutrients for worms and other things shorebirds feed on. . . . It is something that needs to be looked at and studied, but it might be possible to use the ponies in my wildlife management practices. (Personal communication, May 21, 2010)

People like easy explanations and cause-effect relationships. Ecology, however, involves a complex, ever-changing web of relationships, many of which are poorly understood. A change in one part of the web can cause unexpected problems in another part.

The marsh snail (or marsh periwinkle, *Littoraria irrorata*) is found in salt marshes all along the Atlantic coast and is most abundant—as many as 1,500 snails per square meter—in "die-back" zones, where large areas of *Spartina* are dead or dying. This predilection led ecologists to conclude that *Littoraria* is a detritivore that feeds on microorganisms that live on decomposing plants. As it turns out, the snails were actually causing the die-offs to supply themselves with food. Grazing *Littoraria* damage the stalks of live cordgrass, creating lesions that become infected by the fungus that is their primary food. In this way the snails cultivate crops of nutritious fungi, fertilizing it with their dung. Snail grazing and fungus growth kill the cordgrass and causes marsh die-offs. Crabs preying on the snails keep the population in check, minimizing die-offs. Overharvesting blue crabs may be an important contributor to die-offs. Horses also eat cordgrass, but without destroying it, and their grazing thwarts die-offs by increasing the population of crabs and limiting the population of *Littoraria* snails.

When one component of an ecosystem veers off-balance, other components are affected. Until recently, the grazing of lesser snow geese (*Chen caerulescens caerulescens*) strongly benefitted south-central salt marsh communities. These geese spend their summers grazing the Hudson Bay lowlands, then each fall migrate along the Mississippi and Central flyways to winter in Texas and Louisiana. When the geese were surveyed 30 years ago, 600,000 of them grazed these southern marshes and fertilized them with their nitrogen-rich excrement, causing plants to quickly regenerate. Goose population size was limited by the availability of food in the Gulf salt marshes. When farmers along the migration route began using nitrogen fertilizer and high-yield crops in the 1960s, lesser snow geese stopped to feed on corn, soybeans, and wheat, and their reproductive rate sharply increased. Many of these birds began to winter in Arkansas and Missouri, foraging on crops, and many more survived the winter. Today, the census counts 3 million birds, which is probably half the actual total. After gorging on grains all winter, the birds return to the Hudson Bay area to breed alongside Canada geese and destroy the vegetation in the marsh above and below ground. A single goose can strip a square meter (10.8 ft^2) of marsh in an hour, creating a barren mudflat that is unlikely to recover while occupied by geese.

Historically, the Atlantic flowed directly into Currituck Sound via inlets, creating a high-salinity estuarine habitat favorable to oysters and eelgrass and a nursery for saltwater fish. When the three closest inlets—New Currituck, Caffeys, and Roanoke—closed between 1795 and 1828, Currituck Sound became an estuary of increasingly fresh water fed by the tannin-rich rivers draining the Great Dismal Swamp. Shellfish beds disappeared, and sunlight filtered down through the shallow waters and encouraged the growth of aquatic vegetation such as wild celery and wigeon grass. Migrating waterfowl, always plentiful, flocked to this banquet until they literally blackened the sky in a phenomenon known by the locals as "smoke." Recreational hunters were secretive about the whereabouts of their hunting grounds. An exclusive invitation-only organization known as the Currituck Hunting Club purchased more than 3,000 acres/1,214 ha of waterfowl habitat by 1857. Following the Civil War, word of the bountiful waterfowl had spread, and affluent Northerners established more than 100 hunt clubs within a 50-mi/80-km radius of Currituck Sound. Wealthy and powerful men such as J.P. Morgan and Andrew Carnegie made annual pilgrimages to Currituck Banks to hunt waterfowl, as did hunters and fishermen of lesser means. The economy centered on the waterfowl hunting business, with locals working as guides, offering lodging to hunters, and guarding hunting grounds from poachers.

Currituck's waterfowl population, once seemingly infinite, has taken many devastating hits over the past few centuries. Market hunters shot great numbers of wild ducks for commercial sale, using enormous guns up to 10 ft/3 m in length mounted on flat-bottomed "punt" boats propelled by poles. One shot could slay as many as 100 ducks. Working in a team of about 10, each gunner could kill up to 700 ducks in a single day. Around the turn of 20th century, the seemingly inexhaustible flocks grew sparse, not only around Currituck Sound, but all along the Atlantic Flyway.

Thousands of adult snowy egrets were killed in the breeding season, when their plumes were most beautiful—leaving their chicks to starve in the nest. After Congress tightened restrictions, birds were still shot for the black market and shipped in trunks, suitcases, butter firkins, egg crates, horse trailers, and the carcasses of other animals. In 1902, a raid on one cold-storage house in New York yielded 8,058 snow buntings, 7,607 sandpipers, 5,218 plover, 7,003 snipe, 788 yellow legs, 288 bobolinks, 96 woodcock, 7,560 grouse, 4,385 quail, and 1,756 ducks. Most of these birds were illegally hunted, and fines would have totaled $1,168,315 had they been imposed.

Fashion-conscious women and their hatmakers created a seemingly insatiable demand for feathers, and the rarest and most exotic species fetched the highest prices. Species facing extinction brought the highest prices of all. Even hummingbirds were hunted relentlessly to be sold to European hat manufacturers. In 1911, three London millinery-trade auctions included the plumage from 129,168 egrets, 13,598 herons, 20, 698 birds of paradise, 41,090 hummingbirds, and 9,464 eagles and condors put on the block. Before April 1911, when Governor Dix signed the Bayne law and halted the sale of wild native game in the state of New York, Currituck County saw the slaughter of about 200,000 wild fowl annually. Members of sportsmen's clubs could shoot without limit, often bagging 150 or more birds on a two-day hunting trip. Coveting the money that wealthy sportsmen brought in and fearing the consequences of antagonizing them, local and state governments made no move to limit their excesses.

By 1913, Currituck County had earned a reputation as "the bloodiest slaughter-pen for waterfowl that exists anywhere on the Atlantic Coast" (Hornaday, 1913, p. 292). Hunters plied their trade without bag limits, even during the nesting season, and shipped vast quantities of birds to Northern restaurants and dealers.

Habitat loss and wanton hunting caused the American passenger pigeon (*Ectopistes migratorius*) population to collapse from 5–6 billion birds to ignominious extinction in less than 100 years. It appeared that the waterfowl of the Atlantic Flyway would soon follow suit. When President William McKinley signed the Lacey Act (16 U.S.C. §§ 3371–3378) into law in 1900, it became illegal to

On Currituck Banks, in the early 20th century, multitudes of adult snowy egrets were killed for their feathers during the breeding season, leaving their chicks to starve in the nest. Without legal limits on hunting, the bountiful waterfowl population dropped precipitously in just a few decades.

trade or sell wildlife, and many commercial killing machines were silenced, though illicit market gunning continued for decades. Hunt clubs encouraged the avian population to recover by limiting hunting to strictly defined seasons, creating refuges on key portions of their property, prohibiting spring hunting, and imposing bag limits on game. The National Audubon Society incorporated in 1905 as a grassroots conservation agency. In 1918, the Migratory Bird Treaty Act (16 U.S.C. §§ 703–712) protected over 800 species by making it illegal to possess these birds, alive or dead, intact or in part, including feathers, eggs, and nests. From his 7,000-acre/2,800-ha estate on Mackay Island in Currituck Sound, Joseph Palmer Knapp organized international conservation efforts for migratory waterfowl that became Ducks Unlimited in 1937. Knapp's estate later became Mackay Island NWR.

Besides the challenge of heavy hunting pressures, waterfowl populations have suffered large, mysterious die-offs. By the middle of the 20th century 3,000 tons/2.7 million kg of expended lead shot was piling up in the marshes every year, and it was ingested by waterfowl in great quantities. Roughly 2 million ducks succumbed to lead poisoning every year, and many more became chronically ill and slowly wasted away. The birds of Currituck Sound and Back Bay were afflicted in great numbers—yet hunters opposed legislation that would require nontoxic shot, fearing that it would be more expensive or damage their weapons. Ammunition manufacturers, reluctant to retool to accommodate new materials, also resisted a shift away from lead.

The connection between lead ingestion and waterfowl die-offs was recognized in 1874. Lead shot remained entirely unrestricted until 1975 when hunters were required to use steel shot at locations where more than 5% of the ducks harvested were positive for lead ingestion. In 1986, the secretary of the Interior finally imposed a nationwide ban on lead shot for waterfowl hunting in the United States, which took effect in 1991. This ban reduced mortality from lead poisoning in mallards by 64% in the Mississippi Flyway alone and probably saved about 1.4 million ducks annually in the United States in the first years after its enactment.

In the late 19th century, epizootics also devastated the duck population in California, Utah, and other western states, sometimes leaving more than 1,000 dead birds to the acre (2,500/ha). Outbreaks also occurred in North Carolina and the Chesapeake Bay region. Some killed more than a million birds, and mortality of half that number was not uncommon. The best minds of science could not find a cause, though it appeared that toxins such as the chlorides of calcium and magnesium were responsible. Decades later, in 1930, researchers determined that botulism was the true culprit, and it was somehow related to the multitude of aquatic invertebrates dying on mud flats. As it turns out, *Clostridium botulinum* lives in the wetlands as spores, ready to proliferate under the right conditions. When something shifts the balance and causes a large die-off of invertebrates and other small fauna, *Clostridium* spores germinate and produce toxins. When waterfowl feed on the toxin-ridden remains, they die. The maggots

Through the mid-nineteenth century, waterfowl were so abundant on Currituck Sound that clouds of birds would rise like opaque white smoke from the shallows. At the time, the wild horse population on the Outer Banks was at its peak as well, numbering in the thousands. Clearly, the robust equine herd did not negatively impact the great abundance of birdlife.

that feed on the carcasses also contain high levels of *Clostridium* toxins. Sudden fluctuations in water level, pollution, and agricultural runoff can precipitate an outbreak of avian botulism

Today, waterfowl are challenged by environmental contaminants, invasive plants, and the insidious creep of development. Despite improvements in several water quality elements, submerged vegetation has apparently declined in Currituck Sound and Back Bay since tide locks were removed from the Albemarle and Chesapeake Canal, allowing brackish water from Chesapeake Bay to enter through the Elizabeth River.

Bhattacharyya et al. write,

> Interviews with some field managers—resident and nonresident in the area—indicate a tendency to rationalize land use and range management decisions as though the manipulation of a single species (in this case horses) could rectify a century of environmental degradation that has occurred as a result of multiple disturbance factors. In reality, horses are one of many elements impacting ecosystems, any or all of which may require active management in areas where the land becomes degraded. (2011, p. 624)

Some managers of federal lands reject free-roaming horses out of hand as an invasive exotic species that can only cause damage. Many public land managers are pressured by professional wildlife biologists and wildlife interest groups who themselves are heavily biased against wild horses. Others are more open to solutions that accommodate horses as a *resident* species, native or not.

Although horses and hogs are vastly different species that occupy different ecological niches, the Currituck NWR conservation plan makes no distinction between the two, stating unequivocally that "feral hogs (*Sus scrofa*) and horses (*E. caballus*) have overgrazed areas near Carova Beach to the elimination of habitat for native mammal species" (USFWS, 2008, p. 36). Later in the document, under the heading "Pest Animals," the agency appears less certain: "Animals such as feral horses, feral hogs, and nutria *may* [emphasis added] have an impact on habitat and other species, but the Service does not currently staff or fund the refuge to investigate that impact" (p. 88).

In fact, ongoing research has demonstrated that the horses cause no lasting damage to the refuge. Rheinhardt and Rheinhardt (2004) studied the Currituck Banks herd as it foraged on the refuge and found that the herd (including two donkeys) was well below the carrying capacity of the range. They concluded that horses do affect native vegetation "primarily via cropping and trampling" (2004, p. 258), but any damage is temporary. Horses consumed few forb

A black stallion saunters through a community on the "isolated" reaches of the north beach that consists of a development of opulent beach houses and a small park, fenced to keep horses out.

(herbaceous) species, preferring instead graminoid (grass) species, which "seem to recover from grazing by early summer when primary production is highest" (2004, p. 258).

Photographs presented by McCalpin at the July 27, 2010, hearing on H.R. 5482 (the Corolla Wild Horses Protection Act) showed no evidence of overgrazing in the vicinity of six 16 ft x16 ft/4.9 m x 4.9 m exclosures on refuge property (McCalpin, 2010, July 27). At the 2009 census, only eight members of the 121-horse herd were counted foraging on federal land—a population clearly too small and diffuse to impact the environment to any measurable degree. The Wild Horse Fund argued that over a 3-year period, there were never more than 26 horses counted on Fish and Wildlife Service property (CWHF, 2008). Her testimony in 2011 (*H.R. 306, Corolla Wild Horses Protection Act*, 2011b), included the following figures:

- Before 2006, no official census records were found in CWHF archives. Beginning in 2006, aerial counts were conducted by the CWHF Herd Manager and the CNWR Manager . . .
- 2006—119 horses . . .
- 2007—94 . . . 26 horses on CNWR property; 68 on private property; 0 on NCNERR

- 2008—101 ... 23 horses on CNWR property; 74 on private property; 4 on NCNERR
- 2009—88 ... 0 horses on CNWR property; 84 on private property; 4 on NCNERR.
- 2010—115 ... 35 horses on CNWR property; 71 on private property; 9 on NCNERR

In March 2010, the Currituck NWR fenced two large areas with electrified high-tensile wire to determine the impact horses have on the barrier island environment—143 acres/58 ha in Swan Beach, and 135 acres/55 ha in North Swan Beach. Thirteen horses grazed the North Swan Beach tract at the time the fence was erected. Refuge staff literally built the fence around these horses, trapping them, and then asked the Wild Horse Fund to extricate the animals. Stallings complied, but the evicted horses were displaced into the home ranges of other existing harems.

For days, the expatriate horses battled with the resident band and resisted its efforts to drive them away. Harem stallions clashed violently over mares, sustaining cuts and bruises, and one pregnant mare from the displaced group miscarried a foal that was very close to full term. Another mare, apparently healthy when removed from the exclosure, dramatically lost condition over the next month and was euthanized after an heroic attempt to save her life.

Feral horses occupy a home range and will attempt to return to it if moved. Horses have been known to travel more than 9 mi/15 km to return to a home range. The displaced horses wandered up and down the fence, eating grass near the border of their former home ground, trying to get back in, and competing with other horses for resources in the area to which they were banished.

The Currituck NWR built the exclosures to evaluate how the ecosystem functions in the absence of horses. In actuality, the area surrounding the exclosure was used much more heavily and irregularly by horses than it would have been without the fence. Stallings expressed doubt that the results of this experiment are meaningful: "A 12x12 or 16x16 foot enclosure would provide more accurate results, because it does not displace horses from their home ranges" (personal communication, May 25, 2010). "If a stallion has raised a family in a home range, when removed from the 100 acres he will stay as close to the excluded land as possible and possibly overgraze the borders, whereas

The U.S. Fish and Wildlife Service fenced a 135-acre/55-ha exclosure in Currituck NWR to ascertain whether horses were causing environmental damage. From this photograph, taken in November 2012, it is impossible to determine which side of the fence permits equine access, indicating that horses cause minimal impact. In the September 2012 census, only eight horses were counted on the 3,000 acres/1,200 ha of refuge property accessible to them. The remainder of the 121-member herd were counted on private property. Photograph courtesy of the Corolla Wild Horse Fund.

if the exclusion site were open to horses, the grazing would be more evenly distributed."

Meanwhile, development continues to boom on the northern Banks. Horses graze amid real estate signs that mark where the next homes will be built. Stallings maintains that development poses a greater threat to sensitive species than do horses. "Each house has a septic field and a well," he explained. "The water table is high here. Eventually water quality will become affected, and plants adjacent to septic systems will hold toxins detrimental to the environment" (personal communication, May 25, 2010).

"Horses don't destroy grass," Stallings says. "They mow it to a height of 4–6 inches, which is no different than trimming a shrub at your house to a proper level" (personal communication, May

The beach north of Corolla is no longer an "undiscovered paradise." During the warm season, up to 3,000 vehicles per day cruise up and down the shorefront, and endless rows of trucks park with tailgates to the sea.

25, 2010). Moreover, light grazing stimulates plants to grow lower and denser.

The fence keeps the horses out of the paved and thickly settled village of Corolla, but the problems it was meant to solve remain. Horses are still being hit by vehicles and left to die slowly, only now the vehicles are 4x4s and ATVs on the beach. Three horses were struck by vehicles in 2009. A young foal was hit on the beach by a reckless driver and was euthanized while his mother stood nearby, unwilling to leave him. "Most of the incidents are centered around Carova," says Stallings (personal communication, May 25, 2010).

T-Rex, a Corolla stallion in the prime of his life, was struck by a hit-and-run driver in March 2009. The driver knew that she had hit him, but did not report the accident, leaving him to suffer for many hours, in agonized terror, shaking from the effort to remain upright, until the vet finally came to euthanize him. The driver—a recent college graduate whose parents own a beach house in Carova—owned up to the crime more than *two months* after the incident.

Two months later, Spec, another proud stallion featured in a Wild Horse Fund brochure, was struck and left to suffer. It appears that

Horses feed and nap on the lawn surrounding a community of beach houses near Carova. When development transformed their home ranges into suburban outposts, the animals adapted by using the manicured lawns as a food source. Some of the visitors taking horse tours to view the animals are disappointed to find them lounging in back yards and carports rather than galloping wildly down an empty beach.

ATVs were being used to chase the horse around the beach at 1 or 2 a.m. before one hit him from the side with force enough to snap his leg in two. With his leg dangling by a piece of skin, in unimaginable pain, Spec dragged himself almost a mile (1.6 km) across sand and dunes to return to his band. Spec suffered for hours before he could be euthanized. McCalpin wrote, "Spec did not want to die and he fought and struggled long and hard" (2009, May 24). "It was gut wrenching. It was a waste. It was sickening. He was terrified."

In her first four years as director of the Corolla Wild Horse Fund, McCalpin experienced the deaths of 19 horses. In 2009, a lactating mare almost died of agonizingly painful colic after being fed by a resident. This mare was lucky—she lived. Horses are exceptionally vulnerable to digestive disturbances and cannot vomit. A horse's intestines contain great lengths of loopy, mobile, narrow, winding passages that can easily twist, shift, or become obstructed. Consuming unusual foods, even those enjoyed by domestic horses, can kill a wild horse. A lactating mare died of colic in 2006. Attempts to bottle-feed her newborn colt were unsuccessful, and he died shortly after she did. Then in 2008 another horse died after eating moldy alfalfa hay put out by some well-meaning person. Every death subtracts rare and possibly irreplaceable genes from the herd.

Unintentional killings are heartbreaking enough, but, incomprehensibly, there have also been premeditated shootings. From 2001 to 2008, seven horses were gunned down in cold blood and left to decompose. The shooters are still at large despite a $12,550 reward for information leading to their arrest.

Although it is illegal to approach closer than 50 ft/15 m to a Corolla horse, and a $500 fine awaits anyone who violates the statute, people still ignore the boundaries. In 2009, a mother sat by while her two young boys walked up to a stallion and patted him on his hindquarters, oblivious to the danger of even a casual kick. A mother and father attempted to place their child on the back of an unbroken wild horse for a photograph. A woman walked down the beach alongside a group of mares. A family renting a cottage was charged by a stallion when they approached for pictures. A tour group operator prevented a group of children from shooting at a harem of horses with paintball guns.

Although the Corolla horses are maintained as wildlife, and herd managers do not typically interfere with natural sickness and death, the Wild Horse Fund rescues and rehabilitates wild horses injured by encounters with people. Horses are treated in the wild whenever possible. Some problems are fairly minor, such as the colt with a can stuck on his hoof or the filly with a fishhook caught in her leg. One mare was trapped in a deep rut where she would have drowned if not extricated. Another mare managed to ensnare her head in a tomato cage.

Another horse was trapped in a deep, flooded canal till she was saved by Kimberlee Hoey, president of the board of directors for the Wild Horse Fund. Hoey ran from dock to dock, climbing fences and clawing through heavy brush, pushing the mare with a lunge whip. Determined that the horse would not drown, she forced her to swim north toward the nearest break in the bulkhead and guided her to safety.

As if to intensify pressure on the horses from development and traffic, in December 2013, the Fish and Wildlife Service erected 2.9 mi/4.7 km of 15-gauge, 4-strand, 4-point barbed-wire fence, which connects with an existing 142-acre parcel surrounded by high tensile

As lethal as a gun, but much slower acting, concentrated grain pellets can kill a wild horse geared to digesting high-fiber, low-energy grasses. Here somebody dumped a bag of grain on the ground in Swan Beach, presumably to attract horses and bring them within easy viewing range. The herd manager, with the help of the author, scooped the hazard into plastic bags before any horses were poisoned.

wire electric fence. The combination effectively transformed the entire Swan Beach Unit of Currituck NWR, 1,390 acres/563 ha, ocean to sound, into an exclosure that restricts access by horses and deer, but freely admits destructive feral hogs. The agency's reasoning is elusive. Barbed wire is difficult to see and frequently maims or kills not only horses, but also other wildlife, notably deer and large birds such as owls. Kline (2005) says authoritatively that it "should never be used for horse fencing." The Service strung the fence on uncapped metal t-posts, which pose a risk of impalement. Because the refuge has no regularly assigned staff, this fence cannot be monitored. It is easy to foresee that entangled horses, deer, or off-roaders might suffer for hours or days awaiting help. The Corolla Wild Horse Fund posted a photograph of this fence on Facebook, and within days hundreds of outraged people barraged the agency and local politicians with demands to remove it. Yet the fence still stands.

Volunteers must permanently remove some injured horses from the wild. Once a horse relies on humans for its care or is exposed to the diseases carried by domestic horses, it can never rejoin its wild brethren. Veterinary care is expensive, as are boarding fees. Horses unable to return to the beach must be gentled and trained for months before they are suitable for adoption.

Rescues are resource-intensive. When capturing a Corolla horse, volunteers use steel panels to set up a "chute" to funnel the horse into a trailer. The group surrounds the horse and closes the circle toward the trailer. The horse then takes a 2-hr ride to the Dominion Equine Clinic in Suffolk, Va., a hospital with the staff and experience to manage wild horses. In the past few years, many horses have been saved from certain death, including Uno, Tresie, Sunny, Hope, Croatoan, Manteo, Pomiac, Suerte, Tradewind, Valor, Barb, and Rainbow.

A young black stallion, Edward Teach (a.k.a. "Blackbeard"), was rescued after a bite wound laid open his neck during a fight with a rival stallion. *En route* to Dominion Equine Clinic he kicked 15 dents in the trailer. After more than $2,500 worth of veterinary care, the stallion was healed. Unable to return to the herd, he was trained to saddle by Steve Edwards of Mill Swamp Indian Horses in Smithfield, Va., and was eventually adopted.

Rainbow, a black yearling filly, sustained a puncture wound above her chest. Infection traveled up her neck to within 0.25 in./6 mm of her jugular vein and blew out a hole near her jowl almost the size of a tennis ball. Stallings and CWHF volunteers captured her. Dominion Equine Clinic brought her back to health, improved her nutrition, and used physical therapy to return flexibility to her neck. Visitors can see her at the Island Farm, a living-history site near Manteo.

Suerte, from the Spanish for "lucky," was rescued near death after he had ingested something toxic, perhaps antifreeze. Sunny, another young foal, was orphaned when her mother was stolen by another stallion. Young foals must be bottle-fed every 2 hr, so Stallings took the night shift, sleeping in his truck between feedings. McCalpin says, "These little horses have the strongest will to live that I have ever seen" (2009, August 24).

Sometimes horses are removed for their own good. Croatoan, Red Feather, and Swimmer were all escape artists who would not stay between the fences of the north beach and were likely to be struck by vehicles in town. Croatoan was so thin and weak when he was captured in March 2007, a well-meaning bystander pleaded for

Steve Edwards communes with Tradewind, a once-wild Corolla stallion who enjoys his new career as an long distance trail horse. Edwards, who during the work week is an attorney for Isle of Wight County, Va., uses natural horsemanship methods to train Corolla and Shackleford horses, readying them for adoption or placement in the off-site breeding program. Mill Swamp Indian Horses stands Corolla stallions at stud—service is free to any Corolla mare.

his euthanization because he was "old and hungry" (Edwards, 2008). As it turned out, he was only 11 years old, and with medical attention and good nutrition he achieved robust health. Edwards found him surprisingly easy to train. A few months after his capture, young children were using him in riding lessons, and a 10-year-old student rode him in the 2007 Smithfield Christmas Parade. In 2009, the Horse of the Americas Awards Committee gave 8-year-old Sarah Kerr-Applewhite its Buckaroo Award for her long-distance riding accomplishments on Croatoan.

In 2006 a young stallion was removed from the herd and gelded after he begged a resident for food, then knocked her down and injured her when no food was forthcoming. People had been feeding him, so he grew bold and aggressive. A mare named Baton Rouge was removed because she would bite people who came too close, and she gained a new career as a lesson horse.

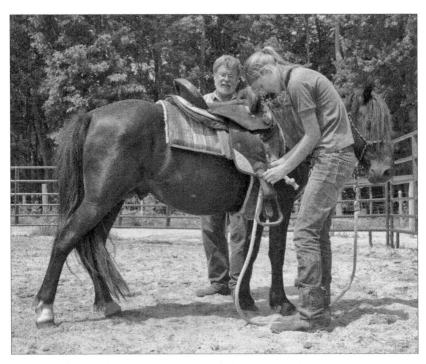

Banker horses transition gratifyingly from beautiful wild creatures to loyal domestic companions. At Mill Swamp Indian Horses in Smithfield, Va., Lydia Barr and Steve Edwards train Edward Teach, a wild-born stallion removed from Currituck Banks after receiving a life-threatening neck wound that has completely healed.

An adoption system places Corolla horses in loving homes from Texas to Maine. Some are maintained in off-site breeding programs so that the Banker Horse might not become extinct if a disease or disaster devastates the island herds. Some are halter-trained before adoption, and some are broken to ride. Martin Community College in Williamston, N.C., trains adoptable Corolla horses as part of its degree program in equine technology. The goal is to place horses in good "forever" homes.

Adopters must demonstrate that they have the knowledge and skills to care for a horse. They are required to provide a shelter or box stall and an outside corral that is at least 20 ft x 20 ft/6 m x 6 m and at least 5 ft/1.5 m high, made of approved, sturdy materials such as pipes or planks. Barbed wire is forbidden because of the horrific injuries a horse may sustain if he becomes entangled. It is easy to adopt a horse in an impulsive emotional rush, but much harder to commit to the daily reality of feeding, watering, cleanup, expense, and meaningful interaction over the long term. A horse can live 20, 30, or even 40-plus years—as much as half a human lifetime.

The legend of Betsy Dowdy's midnight marathon underscores the stamina and heart of the North Carolina Banker Pony. Feats of endurance are well within the repertoire of a marsh pony. Edwards (2011) wrote,

> Exactly what can one expect from a Corolla Colonial Spanish mustang? I can only speak from experience. They are the easiest horses to train with which I have ever worked. They are strong, easy-keeping horses with incredible endurance. Many of our horses have completed rides of 50 miles in a day.
>
> Tradewind, the 2011 Horse of the Americas Registry's National Pleasure Trail Horse of the Year, is a 12.2 hand stallion, weighing 626 pounds in peak condition. In 2011 he carried me 206 hours in the woods, the vast majority of those hours either trotting or cantering. This does not include the many hours that others rode him on the trails. At the time my weight was from 212 to 222 pounds. He did so even though he was captured because he was utterly crippled with founder. He is now wonderfully recovered and has produced two beautiful colts.

The Corolla horse is one of the oldest and rarest strains of Colonial Spanish Horse in the United States. They can trace their ancestry through centuries of free-roaming horses that probably descend from the initial Spanish horses to set hoof in the New World. Other breeds have contributed their genes over the years, but their conformation gives little hint of these introductions. Mill Swamp is one of the off-site breeding farms that raise domestic Banker Horses in an attempt to continue this rare, ancient lineage. Edwards (2011) writes,

> We rehabilitate and train these horses and breed them domestically, not as a replacement for the wild herd, but as a safety net in the event that the wild herd is destroyed by bureaucrats, developers, or a natural catastrophe. The off-site breeding program is designed to insure that these horses, which are the state horse of North Carolina and are among the rarest

and oldest distinct genetic grouping of American horses, will always be with us.

It is equally important, however, to preserve this breed as free-roaming. Wesley Stallings, herd manager, believes that a designated wild horse sanctuary would be an optimal solution. He envisions a fenced area that limits the wild horse range to the marsh, maritime forest, and high ground such as Penny Hill. The marsh would meet the majority of the horses' nutritional needs. The high dunes would provide the same benefits as the beach—strong breezes and insect relief. The horses would remain safely out of the way of traffic, and the prime beachfront property valued by developers would be available for vacation homes. A greenway or boardwalk could allow people to observe the horses in their natural environment from a safe distance. Admission fees would enable the Corolla Wild Horse Fund to better preserve and maintain the herd.

The Fund works tirelessly to raise public awareness and support of the Corolla wild horse. More than 1,000 schoolchildren petitioned to have the Colonial Spanish Mustang designated the North Carolina state horse, a dream that was realized in 2010.

These horses and their ancestors have ranged freely over the dunes of Currituck County for hundreds of years, and cling to existence in the windswept wilds north of Corolla. "It is their last stand—all that remains of their habitat," says McCalpin (2011, February 28).

These animals owe their liberty to the advocates who have battled so relentlessly on their behalf. With continued providence and careful protection, these beautiful horses can remain free on the shifting sands that cover the bones of their ancestors; but maintaining a viable herd will require deliberate conservation efforts. Says Edwards (2011), "Extinction lasts forever and the clock is ticking."

References

An Act Relating to Fences, and for the Protection of Crops. (1873). NC Sess L 1873 ch 103.

An Act To Place Certain Portions of Currituck County under the State-Wide Stock Law. (1937). NC Sess L 1937 ch 389.

An Act To Place Certain Portions of Dare County under the State-Wide Stock Law. (1935). NC Sess L 1935 ch 263.

Altman, J. (2009). *Cape Lookout National Seashore seabeach amaranth (*Amaranthus pumilus*): 2009 report.* Retrieved from http://www.nps.gov/calo/parkmgmt/upload/Cape Lookout National Seashore Sea Beach Amaranth-2009.pdf

Anderson, E.W. (1993). Prescription grazing to enhance rangeland watersheds. *Rangelands, 15*(1), 31–35.

Anderson, V.D. (2002). Animals into the wilderness: The development of livestock husbandry in the seventeenth-century Chesapeake. *William and Mary Quarterly, 3rd Series, 59*(2), 377–408. Retrieved from http://www.jstor.org/stable/3491742

Andreoni, F. (1998). *Evaluating environmental consequences of feral horses in Guy Fawkes River National Park: A report to National Parks and Wildlife Service.* NR 490 Project. Armidale, New South Wales, Australia: University of New England.

Ashton, A. (2005). *Bark chewing by the wild horses of Guy Fawkes River National Park, NSW: Impacts and causes* (Unpublished B.Sc. honors thesis). University of New England, Armidale, New South Wales, Australia.

Bakker, J.P. (1985). The impact of grazing on plant communities, plant populations and soil conditions on salt marshes. *Vegetatio, 62*(1–3), 391–398.

Barber, D.C., & Pilkey, O.H. (2001). *Influence of grazing on barrier island vegetation and geomorphology, coastal North Carolina.* Paper No. 68-0 given at the Geological Society of America Annual Meeting, November 6, 2001. Retrieved from https://gsa.confex.com/gsa/2001AM/finalprogram/abstract_28327.htm

Barlow, C. (2000). *The ghosts of evolution: Nonsensical fruit, missing partners, and other ecological anachronisms.* New York, NY: Basic Books.

Barth, J.E. (2010). "The sinke of America": Society in the Albemarle borderlands of North Carolina, 1663–1729. *North Carolina Historical Review, 87(1),* 1–27.

Bazely, D.R., & Jefferies, R.L. (1986). Changes in the composition and standing crop of salt-marsh communities in response to the removal of a grazer. *Journal of Ecology, 74*(3), 693–706.

Beever, E.A., & Herrick, J.E. (2006). Effects of feral horses in Great Basin landscapes on soils and ants: Direct and indirect mechanisms. *Journal of Arid Environments, 66*(1), 96–112. doi: 10.1016/j.jaridenv.2005.11.006

Beever, E.A., and Brussard, P. F. (2000). Examining ecological consequences of feral horse grazing using exclosures. *Western North American Naturalist, 60*(3), 236–254.

Bellis, V.J. (1995, May). *Ecology of maritime forests of the southern Atlantic coast: A community profile* (Biological Report 30). Washington, DC: U.S. National Biological Service.

Benot, M.L., Bonis, A., Rossignol, N., & Mony, C. (2011). Spatial patterns in defoliation and the expression of clonal traits in grazed meadows. *Botany, 89*(1), 43–54. doi: 10.1139/B10-082

Bertness, M., Silliman, B.R., & Jefferies, R. (2004). Salt marshes under siege. *American Scientist, 92*(1), 54–61.

Bhattacharyya, J., Slocombe, D.S., & Murphy, S.D. (2011). The "wild" or "feral" distraction: Effects of cultural understandings on management controversy over free-ranging horses (*Equus ferus caballus*). *Human Ecology, 39*(5), 613–625. doi: 10.1007/s10745-011- 9416-9

Bill Summary & Status, 112th Congress (2011–2012), H.R.306: All Congressional Actions. (2012). Retrieved from http://thomas.loc.gov/cgi-bin/bdquery/z?d112:HR00306: @@@X

Bill Summary & Status, 113th Congress (2013–2014), H.R.126: All Congressional Actions. (2013). Retrieved from http://thomas.loc.gov/cgi-bin/bdquery/D?d113:13:./temp/~bdWbBw:@@@X|/home/LegislativeData.php?n=BSS;c=113|

Binkley, C. (2007, August). *The creation and establishment of Cape Hatteras National Seashore: The Great Depression through Mission 66.* Atlanta, GA: U.S. National Park Service, Southeast Regional Office, Cultural Resource Division. Retrieved from http://archive.org/stream/creationestablis00bink#page/n1/mode/2up

Bolen, E.G. Waterfowl management: Yesterday and tomorrow. *Journal of Wildlife Management, 64*(2), 323–335.

Bond, J.F. (1908). Report on an examination of the sand banks along the North Carolina coast. In *Biennial Report of the State Geologist, 1907-1908* (pp. 42–48). Raleigh, NC: E.M. Uzzell.

Bos, D., Bakker, J.P., de Vries, Y., & van Lieshout, S. (2002). Long-term vegetation changes in experimentally grazed and ungrazed back-barrier marshes in the Wadden Sea. *Applied Vegetation Science, 5*(1), 4–54.

Bratton, S.P., & Davison, K. (1987). Disturbance and succession in Buxton Woods, Cape Hatteras, North Carolina. *Castanea, 52*(3), 166–179.

Burney, D.A., & Burney, L.P. (1987). Recent paleoecology of Nags Head Woods on the North Carolina Outer Banks. *Bulletin of the Torrey Botanical Club, 114*(2), 156–168.

Carroll, W.D., Kapeluck, P.R., Harper, R.A., & Van Lear, D.H. (2002, September). Background paper: Historical overview of the southern forest landscape and associated resources. In D.N. Wear & J.G. Greis (Eds.), *Southern forest resource assessment* (General Technical Report SRS-53) (pp. 583–605). Asheville, NC: U.S. Forest Service, Southern Research Station.

Carson, R. (1947). *Chincoteague: A National Wildlife Refuge* (Conservation in Action 1). Washington, DC: U.S. Fish and Wildlife Service. Retrieved from http://digitalcommons.unl.edu/ usfwspubs/1

Chapman, W.R., & Hanson, J.K. (1997, January). *Wright Brothers National Memorial historic resource study.* Atlanta, GA: U.S. National Park Service, Southeast Field Area.

Chater, M. (1926). Motor-coaching through North Carolina. *National Geographic, 49* (5), 475–523.

Chen, H. (2013, June 26). Ellis-van Creveld Syndrome. *Medscape.* Retrieved from http://emedicine.medscape.com/article/943684-overview#a0199

Chincoteague ponies: Good points of diminutive draft horses of the coast islands. (1905, September 17). *Washington Post,* p. E2.

Cobb, C. (1906). Where the wind does the work. *National Geographic, 17*(6), 310–317.

Comberford, N. (1657). *The south part of Virginia, now the north part of Carolina* [Map]. Retrieved from http://digitalgallery.nypl.org/ nypldigital/dgkeysearchdetail.cfm?trg=1&strucID=744285&imag eid=ps_mss_cd18_271&total=1&e=w

Conant, E.K., Juras, R., & Cothran, E.G. (2012). A microsatellite analysis of five colonial Spanish horse populations of the southeastern United States. *Animal Genetics, 43*(1), 53–62. doi: 10.1111/j.1365-2052.2011.02210.x

Congressional Budget Office. (2011, November 9). *Cost estimate: H.R. 306, Corolla Wild Horses Protection Act.* Retrieved from http:// www.cbo.gov/sites/default/files/cbofiles/attachments/hr306.pdf

Corolla Wild Horse Fund. (2008, November). Shackleford 127—Corolla 60. *Wild and Free, 1*(7), 1. Retrieved from http://www. corollawildhorses.com/Images/Newsletter/November 2008 Newsletter.pdf

Corolla Wild Horse Fund. (2013, September 23). *YOUR tax dollars at work on the Outer Banks.* Retrieved from http://www.corollawild-horses.com/tax-dollars-work-outer-banks/

Corolla Wild Horses Protection Act. H.R. 5482, 111th Cong. (2010).

Corolla Wild Horses Protection Act, H.R. 306, 112th Cong. (2011).

Corolla Wild Horses Protection Act, H.R. 126, 113th Cong. (2013).

Cothran, E.G. (2008). *Analysis of genetic diversity in the Corolla feral horse herd of North Carolina.* Retrieved from http://www.

A hiker walks past driftwood sculptures crafted by some artistic visitor on the empty, wild beach at Back Bay NWR in Virginia. Wild horses sometimes range into the refuge through False Cape State Park despite the barrier erected to discourage them.

corollawildhorses.com/Images/News/genetic-diversity-analysis. pdf

Cothran, E.G. (2011, April 20). Personal communication.

Cothran, E.G. (2014, September 10). Personal communication.

County of Currituck. (2007). Currituck Banks wild horse management plan: *Final cooperative plan among Currituck County, Corolla Wild Horse Fund, North Carolina Department of Environment and Natural Resources and U.S. Fish and Wildlife Service*. Currituck, NC: Author.

Creecy, R.B. (1901). The legend of Betsy Dowdy: An historical tradition of the Battle of Great Bridge. *North Carolina Booklet, 1*(5).

Currituck County Wild Horse Advisory Board. (2008, October 16). *Currituck County Wild Horse Advisory Board Meeting, October 16, 2008* [Minutes]. Retrieved from http://co.currituck.nc.us/pdf/wild-horse-advisory-board-2008-2011/wh-minutes-08oct16.pdf

Currituck Outer Banks wild horse management plan. (n.d.). Retrieved from http://www.corollawildhorses.com/wp-content/uploads/2012/08/wild-horse-management-plan.pdf

Daniels, J.T. (Photographer). (1903, December 17). *First flight, 120 feet in 12 seconds, 10:35 a.m.; Kitty Hawk, North Carolina.* Library of Congress, Prints & Photographs Division, LC-DIG-ppprs-00626.

De Bry, T. (Engraver). (1590). The arriual of the Englishemen in Virginia. In T. Harriot, *A briefe and true report of the new found land of Virginia* (plate 2). Frankfurt-am-Main, Germany: Johann Wechel.

DeKimpe, N.M., Dolan, R., & Hayden, B.P. (1991). Predicted dune recession on the Outer Banks of North Carolina, USA. *Journal of Coastal Research, 7*(2), 451–463. http://www.jstor.org/stable/4297850

De Stoppelaire, G.H., Gillespie, T.W., Brock, J.C., & Tobin, G.A. (2004). Use of remote sensing techniques to determine the effects of grazing on vegetation cover and dune elevation at Assateague Island National Seashore: Impact of horses. *Environmental Management, 34*(5), 642–649. doi: 10.1007/s00267-004-0009-x

DeBlieu, J. (1998). *Hatteras journal.* Winston-Salem, NC: John F. Blair (Original work published 1987).

Dolan, R., & H. Lins. (1987). Beaches and barrier islands. *Scientific American, 257*(1), 68–77. doi: 10.1038/scientificamerican0787-68

Donlan, C.J., Berger, J., Bock, C.E., Bock, J.H., Burney, D.A., Estes, J.A., . . . Greene, H.W. (2006). Pleistocene rewilding: An optimistic agenda for twenty-first century conservation. *American Naturalist, 168*(5), 660–681. doi: 10.1086/508027

Dunbar, G.S. (1958). *Historical geography of the North Carolina Outer Banks.* Louisiana State University Studies, Coastal Studies Series 3. Baton Rouge: Louisiana State University Press.

Duncan, P., & D'Herbes, J.M. (1982). The use of domestic herbivores in the management of wetlands for waterbirds in the Camargue, France. In D.A. Scott (Ed.), *Managing wetlands and their birds: A manual of wetland and waterfowl management. Proceedings of the third Technical Meeting on Western Palearctic Migratory Bird Management* (pp. 51–56). Slimbridge, United Kingdom: International Waterfowl Research Bureau.

Dyring, J. (1990). *The impact of feral horses (*Equus caballus*) on subalpine and montane environments* (Unpublished master's thesis). University of Canberra, Australia.

Eberhardt, L.L. (2002). A paradigm for population analysis of long-lived vertebrates. *Ecology, 83*(10), 2841–2854.

Edwards, S. (2008, November 24). Croatoan. *Mill Swamp Indian Horse Views*. Retrieved from http://msindianhorses.blogspot.com/search?q=croatoan

Edwards, S. (2011, December 3). Wild Spanish mustangs in Corolla. *Mill Swamp Indian Horse Views*. Retrieved from http://msindianhorses.blogspot.com/2011/12/wild-spanish-mustangs-in-corolla.html

Equus Survival Trust. (2011). *Equus Survival Trust 2011 equine conservation list*. Retrieved from http://www.equus-survival-trust.org/documents/equineconservationlist.pdf

Evans, C. (1986). *The relationship of cattle grazing to sage-grouse use of meadow habitat on the Sheldon National Wildlife Refuge* (Unpublished master's thesis). University of Nevada, Reno.

Farrell, C.A. (n.d.) (Photographer). *One of the great dunes at Kitty Hawk, anchored with brush fence and coarse grass*. PhC9_2_72_21, Charles A. Farrell Photograph Collection, State Archives of North Carolina, Raleigh, NC.

Federal Writers' Project. (1939). *North Carolina: A guide to the Old North State*. Chapel Hill: University of North Carolina Press.

Fishing horses. (1900). *Chambers's Journal, 6th Series* (3), 493.

Friedman, S.M. (n.d.). *The inflation calculator*. Retrieved from http://www.westegg.com/inflation/

Gabriel, A.O., & Kreutzwiser, R.D. (2000). Conceptualizing environmental stress: A stress-response model of coastal sandy barriers. *Environmental Management, 25*(1), 53–69.

Goodloe, R.B., Warren, R.J., Osborn, D.A., & Hall, C. (2000). Population characteristics of feral horses on Cumberland Island, Georgia and their management implications. *Journal of Wildlife Management, 64*(1), 114–121. doi: 10.2307/3802980

Goodwin, D. (2002). Horse behaviour: Evolution, domestication and feralisation. In N. Waran (Ed.), *The Welfare of Horses* (pp. 1–18). Dordrecht, Netherlands: Kluwer Academic Publishers.

Gordon, I., & Duncan, P. (1988). Pastures new for conservation. *New Scientist, 117*(1604), 54–59.

Green, P. (1937). *The Lost Colony: A symphonic drama in two acts (with music, pantomime, and dance)*. Chapel Hill: University of North Carolina Press.

Gura, T. (2012). Genomics, plain and simple. *Nature, 483*(7387), 20–22. doi: 10.1038/483020a

H.R. 306, Corolla Wild Horses Protection Act . . . Legislative hearing before the Subcommittee on Fisheries, Wildlife, Oceans and Insular Affairs of the Committee on Natural Resources, U.S. House of Representatives, 112th Cong. 19 (2011a) (testimony of Michael Hutchins).

H.R. 306, Corolla Wild Horses Protection Act . . . Legislative hearing before the Subcommittee on Fisheries, Wildlife, Oceans and Insular Affairs of the Committee on Natural Resources, U.S. House of Representatives, 112th Cong. 23 (2011b) (testimony of Karen H. McCalpin).

H.R. Doc. No. 1447 at 5307 (1913a).

H.R. Doc. No. 1447 at 5317 (1913b).

H.R. Rep. No. 112-210 (2011).

Haile, J., Froese, D.G., MacPhee, R.D.E., Roberts, R.G., Arnold, L.J., Reyes, A.V., . . . Willerslev, E. (2009). Ancient DNA reveals late survival of mammoth and horse in interior Alaska. *Proceedings of the National Academy of Sciences of the United States of America, 106*(52), 22352–22357. doi: 10.1073/pnas.0912510106

Hampton, J. (2001, November 27). Gunshots kill 3 wild horses. *Virginian-Pilot* (Norfolk, VA), p. B1.

Hampton, J. (2009, July 12). New N.C. law designed to keep visitors, wild horses safe. *Virginian-Pilot* (Norfolk, VA). Retrieved from http://hamptonroads.com/2009/07new-nc-law-designed-keep-visitors-wild-horses-safe

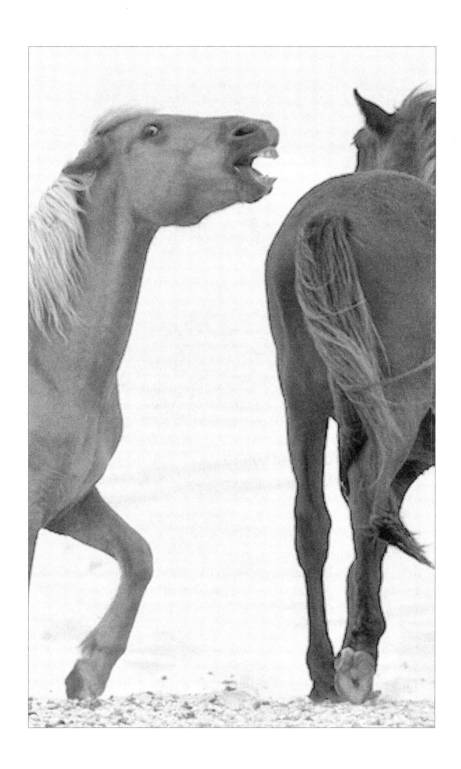

Corolla

Hampton, J. (2013, September 11). Currituck refuge wants more fencing to block wild horses. *Virgininan-Pilot* (Norfolk, VA), p. B5.

Harriot, T. (1590). *A briefe and true report of the new found land of Virginia*. Frankfurt-am-Main, Germany: Johann Wechel.

Harrison, F. (1927). The equine F F Vs: A study of the evidence for the English horses imported into Virginia before the Revolution. *Virginia Magazine of History and Biography, 35*(4), 329–370.

Havholm, K.G., Ames, D.V., Whittecar, G.R., Wenell, B.A., Riggs, S.R., Jol, H.M., . . . Holmes, M.A. (2004). Stratigraphy of back-barrier coastal dunes, northern North Carolina and southern Virginia. *Journal of Coastal Research, 20*(4), 980–999.

Hawks, F.L. (1857). *History of North Carolina: With maps and illustrations* (2nd ed., vol. 1). Fayetteville, NC: E.J. Hale & Son.

Hennigar, H.F. (1979). *Historical evolution of coastal sand dunes on Currituck Spit, Virginia/North Carolina* (Unpublished master's thesis). College of William and Mary, School of Marine Science, Williamsburg, VA.

Henning, J. (1985). *Conquistadores' legacy: The horses of Ocracoke*. Ocracoke, NC: Author.

Hinds, L. (2010, May 21). Personal communication.

Hobbs, N. (1996). Modification of ecosystems by ungulates. *Journal of Wildlife Management, 60*(4), 695–713.

Hobbs, R.J., & Huennecke, L.F. (1992). Disturbance, diversity, and invasion: Implications for conservation. *Conservation Biology, 6*(3), 324–337. doi: 10.1046/j.1523-1739.1992.06030324.x

Hornaday, W.T. (1913). *Our vanishing wild life: Its extermination and preservation.* New York, NY: Charles Scribner's Sons.

Howard, M. (1976). Ocracoke horsemen. In C. O'Neal, A. Rondthaler, & A. Fletcher (Eds.), *The story of Ocracoke Island: A Hyde County bicentennial project* (pp. 25–27). Charlotte, NC: Herb Eaton.

Hutchins, M., et al. (2012, May 1). [Letter to Sen. Barbara Boxer and Sen. James Inhofe.] Retrieved from http://www.publicland.org/08_current_past_news/2012/120501_wild_horse_protection_act.pdf

Impact Assessment, Inc. (2005). *Ethnohistorical description of the eight villages adjoining Cape Hatteras National Seashore and interpretive themes of history and heritage: Final technical report.* Manteo, NC: Cape Hatteras National Seashore.

Jensen, A. (1985). The effect of cattle and sheep grazing on salt-marsh vegetation at Skallingen, Denmark. *Vegetatio, 60*(1), 37-48.

Johnson, K.T. (2006). Fences. *NCPedia.* Retrieved from http://ncpedia.org/fences

Kaczensky, P., Ganbaatar, O., Altansukh, N., & Enkhsaikhan, N. (2010, August). *Winter disaster in the Dzungarian Gobi—Crash of the Przewalski's horse population in Takhin Tal 2009/2010.* Retrieved from http://www.takhi.org/media/forschung/2010_Winter- disaster-in-Dzungarian-Gobi-2009_10.pdf

Keiper, R.R. (1981). *Ecological impact and carrying capacity of ponies.* Contract number 51570–0055. Chincoteague, VA: Chincoteague National Wildlife Refuge.

Kennish, M.J. (2001). Coastal salt marsh systems in the U.S.: A review of anthropogenic impacts. *Journal of Coastal Research, 17*(3), 731–748.

Kirkpatrick, J. (2011, April 12). Personal communication.

Kirkpatrick, J. (2014, May 28). Personal communication.

Kirkpatrick, J., & Fazio, P. (2010, January). *Wild horses as native North American wildlife.* Retrieved from http://awionline.org/content/wild-horses-native-north-american-wildlife

Kline, K. (2005, April 18). *Safe fencing for horses.* Retrieved from http://www.livestocktrail.illinois.edu/horsenet/paperDisplay.cfm?ContentID=6727

Kohn, E. (2004). Can we save the historic Abaco wild horses? *Natural Horse Magazine, 6*(3). Retrieved from http://www.naturalhorse. com/archive/volume6/Issue3/article_8.php

Lacey Act of 1900, 16 U.S.C. §§ 3371–3378 (2006 & Supp. II 2008).

Lamoot, I. (2004). *Foraging behaviour and habitat use of large herbivores in a coastal dune landscape.* Brussels, Belgium: Research Institute for Nature and Forest. Retrieved from http://www.inbo. be/files/bibliotheek/14/167914.pdf

Lawson, J. (1709). *A new voyage to Carolina; Containing the exact description and natural history of that country. . . .* London, United Kingdom. Retrieved from http://docsouth.unc.edu/nc/lawson/ lawson.html

Lee, F.G. (2008). *Constructing the Outer Banks: Land use, management, and meaning in the creation of an American place* (Unpublished master's thesis). North Carolina State University, Raleigh.

Lellis, K.A. (2008). *Native Phragmites australis in national parks: A three-step approach to locate, identify, and verify native stands of the common reed in the northeast* (CIIP White Paper). Retrieved from http://www.ci.uri.edu/ciip/WhitePaper/2008/ Lellis.pdf

Levin, P., Ellis, J., Petrik, R., & Hay, M. (2002). Indirect effects of feral horses on estuarine communities. *Conservation Biology, 16*(5), 1364–1371. doi: 10.1046/j.1523-1739. 2002.01167.x

Lloyd, J. (2013, February 13). *The story of the rise and fall of the Currituck hunt clubs.* http://www.ncbeaches.com/Features/Wildlife/HistoryofCurrituckHuntClubs

Locke, L.N., & Friend, M. (1989). *Avian botulism: Geographic expansion of a historic disease* (Fish and Wildlife Leaflet 13.2.4). Washington, DC: U.S. Fish and Wildlife Service.

Loydi, A., & Zalba, S.M. (2009). Feral horses dung piles as potential invasion windows for alien plant species in natural grasslands. In A.G. van der Valk (Ed.), *Herbaceous Plant Ecology* (pp. 107–116). doi: 10.1007/978-90-481-2798-6

Lynghaug, F. (2009). *The official horse breeds standards guide: The complete guide to the standards of all North American equine breed associations.* Minneapolis, MN: Voyageur Press.

MacNeil[l], B.D. (1938, June 14). Dare sharpshooters begin Banker Ponies' extinction. *News and Observer* (Raleigh, NC), p. 1.

MacNeill, B.D. (1958). *The Hatterasman.* Winston-Salem, NC: John F. Blair.

Mallinson, D.J., Culver, S.J., Riggs, S.R., Walsh, J.P., Ames, D., & Smith, C.W. (2008). *Past, present and future inlets of the Outer Banks barrier islands, North Carolina.* Greenville, NC: East Carolina University.

Mallinson, D.J., Riggs, S.R., Culver, S.J., Ames, D., Horton, B.P., & Kemp, A.C. (2009). *The North Carolina Outer Banks barrier islands: A field trip guide to the geology, geomorphology, and processes.* Retrieved from http://core.ecu.edu/geology/mallinsond/IGCP_NC_Field_Trip_Guide_rev1.pdf

Marion, J.L. (2010). Management, monitoring, and protection protocols for seabeach amaranth at Cape Hatteras National Seashore, North Carolina. In *A review and synthesis of the scientific information related to the biology and management of species of special concern at Cape Hatteras National Seashore, North Carolina* (Open-File Report 2009–1262) (pp. 89–100). Reston, VA: U.S. Geological Survey.

McCalpin, K. (2009, August 24). Sunny and Suerte. *Wild and Free Weekly.* Retrieved from http://corollawildhorses.blogspot.com/2009/08/sunny-and-suerte.html

McCalpin, K. (2009, June 29). Killing them softly. *Wild and Free Weekly*. Retrieved from http://corollawildhorses.blogspot.com/2009_06_01_archive.html

McCalpin, K. (2009, May 24). Another senseless death. *Wild and Free Weekly*. Retrieved from http://corollawildhorses.blogspot.com/2009/05/another-senseless-death.html

McCalpin, K. (2010, March 2). Horses or hotel? *Wild and Free Weekly*. Retrieved from http://corollawildhorses.blogspot.com/2010/03/

horses-or-hotel.html

McCalpin, K. (2010, March 24). HB 4867—The Corolla Wild Horse Protection Act. *Wild and Free Weekly*. Retrieved from http://corollawildhorses.blogspot.com/2010/03/hb-4867-corolla-wild-horse-protection.html

McCalpin, K. (2010, June 16). Our fragile home. *Wild and Free Weekly*. Retrieved from http://corollawildhorses.blogspot.com/2010_06_01_archive.html

McCalpin, K. (2011, February 28). They paved paradise and put up a parking lot . . . *Wild and Free Weekly*. Retrieved from http://corollawildhorses.blogspot.com/2011/02/they-paved-paradise-and-put-up-parking.html

McCalpin, K. (2011, March 21). The height of stupidity. *Wild and Free Weekly*. Retrieved from http://corollawildhorses.blogspot.com/2011/03/height-of-stupidity.html

McCalpin, K. (2011, April 13). We asked for wild horses—not elephants! *Wild and Free Weekly*. Retrieved from http://corollawildhorses.blogspot.com/2011/04/we-asked-for-wild-horses-not-elephants.html

McCalpin, K.H. (2010). *Saving the horses of kings: The wild horses of the Currituck Outer Banks*. Kitty Hawk, NC: Outer Banks Press.

McCalpin, K.H. (2010, July 27). *Hearing on H.R. 5482 Corolla Wild Horses Protection Act, U.S House of Representatives, Subcommittee on Insular Affairs, Oceans, and Wildlife: Testimony of Karen H. McCalpin, Executive Director, Corolla Wild Horse Fund, Inc. Corolla, North Carolina*. Retrieved from http://naturalresources.house.gov/UploadedFiles/McCalpinTestimony07.27.10.pdf

McGowan, C.P., & Simons, T.R. (2006). Effects of human recreation on the incubation behavior of American oystercatchers. *Wilson Journal of Ornithology, 118*(4), 485–493.

Mead, J.G. (1975). Preliminary report on the former net fisheries for *Tursiops truncatus* in the western North Atlantic. *Journal of the Fisheries Research Board of Canada, 32*(7): 1155–1162. doi: 10.1139/f75-136

Menard, C., Duncan, P., Fleurance, G., Georges, J.Y., & Lila, M. (2002). Comparative foraging and nutrition of horses and cattle in European wetlands. *Journal of Applied Ecology, 39*(1), 120–133. doi: 10.1046/j.1365-2664.2002.00693.x

Migratory Bird Treaty Act of 1918, 16 U.S.C. §§ 703–712 (2006).

Mills, D.S., & McDonnell, S.M. (Eds.). (2005). *The domestic horse: The evolution, development and management of its behaviour.* Cambridge University Press.

Mitchell, L.R. Gabrey, S., Marra, P.O., & Erwin, M.R. (2006). Impacts of marsh management on coastal-marsh bird habitats. *Studies in Avian Biology, 32,* 155–175.

Mysterud, A. (2006). The concept of overgrazing and its role in management of large herbivores. *Wildlife Biology, 12*(2), 129–141.

National Research Council. (2013). *Using Science to Improve the BLM Wild Horse and Burro Program: A way forward.* Washington, DC: The National Academies Press.

Nimmo, D.G., & Miller, K.K. (2007). Ecological and human dimensions of management of feral horses in Australia: A review. *Wildlife Research, 34*(5), 408–417. doi: 10.1071/WR06102

Oduor, A.M.O., Gómez, J.M., & Strauss, S.Y. (2010). Exotic vertebrate and invertebrate herbivores differ in their impacts on native and exotic plants: A meta-analysis. *Biological Invasions, 12*(2), 407–419. doi: 10.1007/s10530-009-9622-1

Outer Banks Conservationists. [2008]. *Currituck Beach Lighthouse: Chronological list of keepers, 1875–2006.* Retrieved from http://www.currituckbeachlight.com/ ChronologicalListofCBLHkeepers.pdf

Owens, G. (2008, January 21). *Reward offered in wild horse shootings.* Retrieved from http://www.wral.com/news/local/story/2334908/

Pease, M.L., Rose, R.K., & Butler, M.J. (2005). Effects of human disturbances on the behavior of wintering ducks. *Wildlife Society Bulletin, 33*(1), 103–112.

Pendleton, E.A., Thieler, E.R., & Williams, S.J. (2004). *Coastal vulnerability assessment of Cape Hatteras National Seashore (CAHA) to sea-level rise* (U.S. Geological Survey Open-File Report 2004-1064). Retrieved from http://pubs.usgs.gov/of/2004/1064/images/pdf/caha.pdf

Pidgin, C.F. (1907). *Theodosia: The first gentlewoman of her time.* Boston, MA: C.M. Clark.

Pilkey, O.H., Neal, W.J., Riggs, S.R., Webb, C.A., Bush, D.M., Pilkey, D.F, . . . Cowan, B.A. (1998). *The North Carolina shore and its barrier islands: Restless ribbons of sand.* Durham, NC: Duke University Press.

Pilkey, O., Rice, T., & Neal, W. (2004). *How to read a North Carolina beach*. Chapel Hill: University of North Carolina Press.

Plassmann, K., Jones, M.L.M., & Edwards-Jones, G. (2010). Effects of long-term grazing management on sand dune vegetation of high conservation interest. *Applied Vegetation Science, 13*(1), 100–112. doi: 10.1111/j.1654-109X.2009.01052.x

Poney Penning on the Beach, Near Oriental, N.C. (*ca.* 1910). In Durwood Barbour Collection of North Carolina Postcards (P077), North Carolina Collection Photographic Archives, Wilson Library, University of North Carolina-Chapel Hill.

Prioli, C. (2007). *The wild horses of Shackleford Banks*. Winston-Salem, NC: John F. Blair.

Quinn, D.B. (Ed.) (1955). *The Roanoke voyages, 1584–1590: Documents to illustrate the English voyages to North America under the patent granted to Walter Raleigh in 1584*. London, United Kingdom: For the Hakluyt Society.

Re: Denial of request to allow Corolla wild Colonial Spanish Mustangs to remain at a genetically healthy level. (2008). Retrieved from http://www.corollawildhorses.com/Images/News/genetic-crisis-rev.pdf

Reeves, R.R., & Mitchell, E. (1988, March). *History of whaling in and near North Carolina*. NOAA Technical Report NMFS 65. Washington, DC: National Oceanic and Atmospheric Administration, National Marine Fisheries Service.

Rehor, M. (2014, February 17). Personal communication.

Reiner, R.J., & Urness, P.J. (1982). Effect of grazing horses managed as manipulators of big game winter range. *Journal of Range Management, 35*(5), 567–571.

Rheinhardt, R.D., & Rheinhardt, M.C. (2004). Feral horse seasonal habitat use on a coastal barrier spit. *Journal of Range Management, 57*(3), 253–258.

Rogers, G. (1994, August). *Kaimanawa feral horses: Recent environmental impacts in their northern range*. Landcare Research Contract Report: LC 9495121. Hamilton, New Zealand: Manaaki Whenua—Landcare Research.

Rogers, G.M. (1991). Kaimanawa feral horses and their environmental impacts. *New Zealand Journal of Ecology, 15*(1), 49–64.

Rubenstein, D.R., Rubenstein, D.I., Sherman, P.W., & Gavin, T.A. (2006). Pleistocene Park: Does re-wilding North America represent sound conservation for the 21st century? *Biological Conservation, 132*(2), 232–238. doi: 10.1016/j.biocon.2006.04.003

Russell, D.A., Rich, F.J., Schneider, V., & Lynch-Steiglitz, J. (2009). A warm thermal enclave in the Late Pleistocene of the Southeastern United States. *Biological Reviews, 84*(2), 173–202. doi: 10.1111/j.1469-185X.2008.00069.x

Sanders, A.E. (2002). Additions to the Pleistocene mammal faunas of South Carolina, North Carolina, and Georgia. *Transactions of the American Philosophical Society, 92*, Part 5.

Schott, C. (2002). Ecology of free-ranging horse in northern Guy Fawkes River National Park—Research progress report. Armidale, New South Wales, Australia: University of New England.

Scorolli, A.L. (2012). Feral horse body condition: A useful tool for population management? In *International Wild Equid Conference, Vienna 2012: Book of abstracts* (p. 92). Vienna, Austria: Research Institute of Wildlife Ecology, University of Veterinary Medicine. Retrieved from http://www.vetmeduni.ac.at/fileadmin/v/fiwi/Konferenzen/Wild_Equid_Conference/IWEC_book_of_abstracts_final.pdf

Seliskar, D.M. (2003). The response of *Ammophila breviligulata* and *Spartina patens* (Poaceae) to grazing by feral horses on a dynamic Mid-Atlantic barrier island. *American Journal of Botany, 90*(7), 1038–1044

Senter, J. (2003). Live dunes and ghost forests: Stability and change in the history of North Carolina's maritime forests. *North Carolina Historical Review, 80*(3), 334–361.

Severson, K.E., & Urness, P.J. (1994). Livestock grazing: A tool to improve wildlife habitat. In M. Vavra, W.A. Laycock, & R.D. Pieper (Eds.), *Ecological implications of livestock herbivory in the West* (pp. 232–249). Denver: Society for Range Management.

Shomette, D.G. (2008). The price of amity: Of wrecking, piracy, and the tragic loss of the 1750 Spanish treasure fleet. *The Northern Mariner/le marin du nord, 18*(3–4), 25–48.

Sloan, K. (2007). *A new world: England's first view of America.* Chapel Hill: University of North Carolina Press.

Smith, C.G., Culver, S.J., Riggs, S.R., Ames, D., Corbett, D.R., & Mallinson, D. (2008). Geospatial analysis of barrier island width of two segments of the Outer Banks, North Carolina, USA: Anthropogenic curtailment of natural self-sustaining processes. *Journal of Coastal Research, 24*(1), 70–83. doi: 10.2112/05-0595.1

Spears, J.R. (1890, October). Sand-waves at Henlopen and Hatteras. *Scribner's Magazine, 8*(4), 507–512.

Stallings, W. (2010, May 25). Personal communication.

Stewart, M.A. (1991). "Whether wast, deodand, or stray": Cattle, culture, and the environment in early Georgia. *Agricultural History, 65*(3), 1–28.

Stick, D. (1958). *The Outer Banks of North Carolina, 1584–1958.* Chapel Hill: University of North Carolina Press.

Stroh, P.A., Mountford, J.O., & Hughes, F.M.R. (2012). The potential for endozoochorous dispersal of temperate fen plant species by free-roaming horses. *Applied Vegetation Science, 15*(3), 359–368. doi: 10.1111/j.1654-109X.2011.01172.x

Taggart, J.B. (2008). Management of feral horses at the North Carolina Estuarine Research Reserve. *Natural Areas Journal, 28*(2), 187–195.

Take the trip of a lifetime! (2009). Retrieved from http://www.corollawildhorses.com/trip_of_a_lifetime.html

Tate, W. (1900, August 18). Letter to Wilbur Wright. Retrieved from http://www.bsu.edu/eft/wright/p/library/letter6.html

Taylor, U. (1995). *Seed dispersal from feral horse manure at Guy Fawkes River National Park.* NR 490 Project. Armidale, New South Wales, Australia: University of New England.

Tennant, D. (2001, December 2). Swept away: Shifting sands cover what once was Seagull, N.C. *Virginian-Pilot* (Norfolk, VA), p. E1.

Tennis, J. (2009, September 13). *Home on the range.* Retrieved from http://www.tricities.com/news/article_09b7b5d3-bd47-5d18-80e4-5b20bc9cbf52.html

Tesauro, J., & Ehrenfeld, D. (2007). The effects of livestock grazing on the bog turtle [*Glyptemys* (=*Clemmys*) *muhlenbergii*]. *Herpetologica, 63*(3):293-300. doi: 10.1655/ 0018-0831(2007)63[293:TEOLGO] 2.0.CO;2

Tsoar, H. 2005). Sand dunes mobility and stability in relation to climate. *Physica A: Statistical Mechanics and its Applications, 357*(1), 50–56.

Turner, M.G. (1987). Effects of grazing by feral horses, clipping, trampling, and burning on a Georgia salt marsh. *Estuaries, 10*(1), 54–60.

U.S. Bureau of Labor Statistics. (n.d.). *CPI inflation calculator.* Retrieved from http://www.bls.gov/data/inflation_calculator.htm

U.S. Department of Interior. (2010, March). *Draft environmental assessment, 2010 sport hunting plan amendment for Currituck National Wildlife Refuge, Currituck County, North Carolina.* Retrieved from http://www.fws.gov/currituck/images/D4_Envir_Assess.pdf

U.S. Fish and Wildlife Service. (1999, May). *Attwater Prairie Chicken National Wildlife Refuge.* Retrieved from http://library.fws.gov/ Refuges/attwater.pdf

U.S. Fish and Wildlife Service. (2008, November). *Currituck National Wildlife Refuge comprehensive conservation plan.* Atlanta, GA: USFWS Southeast Region.Retrieved from http://digitalmedia.fws. gov/cdm/ref/collection/document/id/397

U.S. Fish and Wildlife Service. (2010, September). *Back Bay National Wildlife Refuge comprehensive conservation plan.* Retrieved from http://www.fws.gov/northeast/   planning/Back%20Bay/pdf/ FinalCCP/BACKBAYNWRFinalCCP9_2010.pdf

U.S. Fish and Wildlife Service. (2012, November 23). *Attwaters prairie-chicken.* Retrieved from http://www.fws.gov/refuge/Attwater_ Prairie_Chicken/wildlife/APC.html

Vavra, M. (2005). Livestock grazing and wildlife: Developing compatibilities. *Rangeland Ecology & Management, 58*(2), 128–134. doi: 10.2111/1551-5028(2005)58<128:LGAWDC>2.0.CO;2

Vega-Pla, J.L., Calderón, J., Rodríguez-Gallardo, P.P., Martínez, A.M., & Rico, C. (2006). Saving feral horse populations: Does it really matter? A case study of wild horses from Doñana National Park in southern Spain. Animal Genetics, 37, 571–578. doi: 10.1111/j.1365-2052.2006.01533.x

Wallace, J.H. (1897). *The horse of America in his derivation, history, and development.* New York, NY: Author.

Weakley, A., Bucher, M., & Murdock, N. (1996). *Recovery plan for seabeach amaranth (*Amaranthus pumilus*) Rafinesque.* Atlanta, GA: U.S. Fish and Wildlife Service. Retrieved from http://pbadupws. nrc.gov/docs/ML0719/ML071970324.pdf

Weaver, V., & Adams, R. (1996). Horses as vectors in dispersal of weeds into bushland. In R.G. Richardson & F.J. Richardson (Eds.), *Eleventh Australian Weeds Conference Proceedings* (pp. 383–387). Frankston, Victoria, Australia: Weed Science Society of Victoria.

White, J. (Artist). (ca. 1585). [Plan of the Grenville expedition's camp at Tallaboa Bay, Puerto Rico] [Watercolor]. London, United Kingdom: British Museum.

Williams, B., & Page, M.P. (2002–2003). Where the feral horses roam. *Roanoke Colonies Research Newsletter, 8*(1 & 2). Retrieved from http://www.ecu.edu/rcro/RCRONLvol8WhereFeralHorsesRoam. htm

Wilson, A.D., & MacLeod, N.D. (1991). Overgrazing: Present or absent? *Journal of Range Management, 44*(5), 475–482.

Wiss, Janney, Elstner Associates & John Milner Associates. (2007). *Portsmouth Village cultural landscape report.* Atlanta, GA: U.S. National Park Service, Southeast Regional Office.

Wolfe, M. (2003, September 20). (Photographer). [Inlet cut through Hatteras Island by Hurricane Isabel]. Retrieved from http://commons.wikimedia.org/wiki/File:FEMA_-_ 8414_-_Photograph_by_ Mark_Wolfe_taken_on_09-20-2003_in_North_ Carolina.jpg

Wolfe, M. (2003, September 23). [(Photographer). Damage from Hurricane Isabel in Kitty Hawk, NC]. Retrieved from http://commons. wikimedia.org/wiki/File:FEMA_-_ 8411_-_Photograph_by_Mark_ Wolfe_taken_on_09-23-2003_in_North_ Carolina.jpg

Wood, G.W., Mengak, M.T., & Murphy, M. (1987). Ecological importance of feral ungulates at Shackleford Banks, North Carolina. *American Midland Naturalist, 118*(2), 236–244.

Woolford, P. (2012, May 9). *At Currituck NWR: No horsing around when it comes to protecting native wildlife.* Retrieved from http://refugeassociation.org/2012/05/at-currituck-nwr-no-horsing-around/

Wylie, D.D.J. (2012). *Vegetation change on San Clemente Island following the removal of feral herbivores* (Unpublished master's thesis). San Diego State University, CA.

Zalba, S.M., & Cozzani, N.C. (2004). The impact of feral horses on grassland bird communities in Argentina. *Animal Conservation, 7*(1), 35–44. doi: 10.1017/S13679430030010

Acknowledgments

About 20 years ago, I began to research my first book, *Hoofprints in the Sand: Wild Horses of the Atlantic Coast*. The experience enriched my life in many ways. I learned a tremendous amount about how the natural behavior of these horses differs from that of their domestic counterparts. Following herds through marsh and dune, I gained a greater appreciation of the complexity of their apparently simple lives in the wild. Similarly, with the writing of *Wild Horse Dilemma*, many helpful and extraordinary people have earned my gratitude, and many have become friends.

Dr. Jay F. Kirkpatrick, senior scientist at the Science and Conservation Center at ZooMontana in Billings and author of *Into the Wind: Wild Horses of North America*, has devoted much of his career to preserving the health, rights, and dignity of wild horses. He developed and implemented the immunocontraceptive program in use with many species of wildlife, including horses. He answered my questions, forwarded useful documents, crafted an insightful preface, and generously reviewed the manuscript before publication.

Don Höglund, DVM, is an internationally esteemed leader in horse training and management and the author of *Nobody's Horses*, a riveting book about the rescue of wild horses from the White Sands Missile Range. He has implemented numerous large-scale equine programs, including the Department of the Interior's Wild Horse Prison Inmate Training Program, which teaches prisoners to gentle horses while providing training for adoptable mustangs. His love and admiration for horses is evident in all that he does. When I approached him with a few questions, he responded enthusiastically and sent me a number of articles that shaped the backbone of my manuscript. I am grateful for his support and encouragement along the way and fortunate that he agreed to review the manuscript.

Dr. E. Gus Cothran, Texas A&M University's renowned expert on the genetics of wild and domestic horses, helped me to understand the significance of the Q-ac variant in certain wild horse herds and the concept of minimum viable population. He also found time in his busy schedule to review the manuscript. His research is the cornerstone of wild horse management, and I have cited it extensively.

Dr. Sue Stuska, the wildlife biologist at Cape Lookout National Seashore who oversees the Shackleford Banks herd, has corresponded regularly about the status of the horses. When I visited, she taught me how to identify individuals, and showed me her dynamic census chart that tracks the members of each band and where they were last sighted. She explained how the current management plan makes optimal use of the existing gene pool by monitoring family lineage and contracepting certain mares. Sue also gave of her valuable time to review my manuscript for accuracy.

Doug Hoffman, wildlife biologist at Cumberland Island National Seashore, helped me to understand the Park Service perspective on the horses living there and corrected my assumptions and misinformation. He generously drove me to key parts of the island that I could not otherwise reach, and my time with him was the highlight of the trip.

Karen McCalpin, director of the nonprofit Corolla Wild Horse Fund, Inc., found time in her impossibly busy schedule to meet me and discuss the genetic crisis facing the herd. She also reviewed the manuscript. Karen and the other members of the organization—mostly volunteers—have upended their lives to secure protection for these horses. Karen produced a beautifully written blog highlighting the triumphs and tragedies of the herd. It can be accessed at www.corollawildhorses.com

Dr. Ronald Keiper, Distinguished Professor of Biology (emeritus) at Penn State University, was one of the first scientists to study the behavior of horses in the wild, answered my questions about the foaling rate of lactating mares and shared his groundbreaking research detailing the behavior of the Assateague horses.

Wesley Stallings, former manager of the Corolla herd, took me in his truck several times as he patrolled the Outer Banks north of Corolla, following the movements of wild bands and logging herd data in his notebook. Sometimes we climbed on the roof of the truck to scout for horses. Sometimes Wes climbed a tree for a better view. At one point we encountered a flooded hollow and were forced to don hip boots and slog through surging currents occupied by cottonmouth snakes

to evaluate the health of a newborn colt. I am grateful he allowed me to participate in his daily adventures.

Steve Edwards, by day an attorney for Isle of Wight County, Virginia, works magic in rehabilitating injured Corolla and Shackleford horses. At his farm, Mill Swamp Indian Horses in Smithfield, Va., he teaches children how to train wild horses with natural horsemanship techniques. He also established an off-site breeding program to preserve the herd's rare genes in case of disaster in the wild. Steve has been extremely supportive and helpful throughout the writing of this book, and has brought his expertise to the task of reviewing this book for accuracy before publication.

In 2012, I visited Mill Swamp and was captivated by the sight of children working in the round pen with young horses, many of them recently brought in from the wild. To this point, I had great esteem for the wild horses living on North Carolina's Outer Banks, but had never ridden one. I found these Colonial Spanish Horses astonishingly surefooted, brave, rugged, and smooth-gaited. The climax of my visit was a ride through the inky forest astride Manteo, a wild-born black stallion. He never missed a step despite exposed roots, steep embankments, deep pools, and deer crashing gracelessly through the underbrush. For the better part of an hour, we trotted and cantered through darkness so complete, I could not see my hand in front of my face. I had recently been injured in a riding accident, and I was working through many horse-related fears. It was a profound and humbling experience to trust a once-wild stallion to find his way through darkness that left me blind.

D. Phillip Sponenberg, DVM, PhD, helped me to understand the genetic underpinnings of coat color and its implications for the free-roaming Banker horses. In his review of the manuscript, he offered great insights on Spanish horse origins and genetics, and his comprehensive articles on that topic were a valuable resource.

Carolyn Mason, president of the Foundation for Shackleford Horses, Inc., accompanied me to Shackleford Banks and generously shared her wealth of knowledge about the horses. She introduced me to the Banker Horses grazing in her yard, gentled animals awaiting adoption. My heart melted when a young gelding named Adagio followed me like a puppy and courted hugs and scratching.

Woody and Nena Hancock loaded me and my cameras into their boat and searched island and marsh for members of the Cedar Island herd. They introduced me to Bucky, the most genetically valuable horse on Cedar Island, and her 2-week-old look-alike filly, Gay; a mare who prefers the company of three burly wild bulls; and Shack, the robust sorrel patriarch whose photograph graces the front cover of this book. It was a profound, almost holy experience to stand calf-deep in warm estuarine waters under a moody sky, surrounded by peaceful wild horses, splashing pelicans, and wind-licked marsh grass.

Laura Michaels, the Park Service ranger in charge of pony care, took me behind the scenes to meet the Ocracoke horses. I also met Wenzel, Doran, Sacajawea, and Jitterbug, the Shackleford horses who will revitalize the Ocracoke herd. I even scratched the neck of the lovely black-and-white mare Easter Lady after admiring her from afar for years.

Roe Terry, former public relations specialist of the Chincoteague Volunteer Fire Company, invited me to the workshop where he carves graceful wooden waterfowl and discussed the challenges faced by the hardworking firefighters. Besides managing the herd of free-roaming ponies, these dedicated people donate their time to provide tax-free fire suppression, search and rescue, and emergency medical services in a town of 4,400 permanent residents that receives roughly 1.5 million visitors a year. He also granted me access to the optimal vantage point for the world-famous Chincoteague Pony Swim: whereas most onlookers stood in a field behind an orange fence, out of harm's way, I was able to stand directly on the grassy landing where the horses regained solid ground after swimming the channel from Chincoteague National Wildlife Refuge. Ponies rose out of the water like mythical creatures of the sea, dripping wet and looking very pleased with themselves. My feet were in their hoofprints, and occasionally I dove for cover as a stallion thundered by in pursuit of a rival. It was a magical experience.

Denise Bowden, his successor at the fire company, cheerfully supplied me with useful information. Her passion for the horses and the refuge are evident, and her enthusiasm enhances the overall festivity of Pony Penning week.

Lou Hinds, former manager of the Chincoteague NWR, took me around the refuge to show me unequivocal signs of dramatic environmental change, such as tree trunks, light poles, and chunks of peat that had once been on the bay side of Assateague until island migration situated them squarely on the beach. Studying the dynamic nature of barrier islands is one thing; seeing the evidence of their migration is another thing entirely.

Pam Emge, co-author of *Chincoteague Ponies: Untold Tails*, can identify all of the Chincoteague wild ponies and knows the intimate details of their relationships and lineages. She reviewed part of the manuscript, corrected errors, and filled in details.

Anthropologist Karen Dalke of the University of Wisconsin-Green Bay shared her doctoral dissertation and other writings, which provide unique perspective on what we feel about wild horses and how we define them. She also reviewed the manuscript prior to publication.

Paula Gillikin, manager of the Rachel Carson North Carolina National Estuarine Research Reserve, assisted me in researching the horses of Carrot Island and vicinity.

Philip Howard, nephew of Marvin Howard (1897–1969), who led Ocracoke's mounted Boy Scout troop in the late 1950s, and grandson of the legendary horseman Homer Howard, allowed me to use excerpts from his Web site detailing his family history with the wild ponies.

Allison Turner, biological science technician at Assateague Island National Seashore, supplied excellent information about the Maryland herd and shared Park Service photographs that vividly show the bites and kicks that occur when people get too close to wild horses.

DeAnna Locke, administrator of the Ocracoke Preservation Society, let me pore over and digitize the organization's fascinating scrapbooks, which included many pictures of the island's mounted Boy Scout troop.

Tim Ferry and Flickr user rich701 allowed me to reprint some of their unique historical photographs of the Chincoteague herd.

Craig Downer, a wild-horse ecologist and activist on the board of directors of the Cloud Foundation, shared several of his writings with me on the subject of mustang management.

Jean Bonde of the Buy-Back Babes has a contagious enthusiasm for the Chincoteague Ponies and many tales to tell. These ponies have a large cult following, and her e-mail group recounted the details of their lives—celebrating the romance of Copper Moose and Scotty's ET, pondering Rip Tide's status within Surfer Dude's band, and speculating on why Queenie and Suzy Sweetheart were wandering around the wildlife loop.

Tabetha Fenton of Barefoot Minis helped with proofreading and offered enthusiastic support.

Special thanks to my mother, Joyce Urquhart, who is an exceptionally good proofreader. She read every word of the manuscript and discovered errors that other readers missed.

My husband, Alex, is committed to giving me space in which to create and assisting me wherever possible in my creative pursuits. Besides proof-reading my manuscripts, he is the behind-the-scenes man who maintains the household, runs to the post office, and brings in the bird feeders at night so the bears don't destroy them. He is the love of my life and I am thankful every day that we are together.

About the Author

Bonnie Urquhart Gruenberg is a multifaceted person who wishes that sleep were optional. She is the author of the award-winning textbook *Birth Emergency Skills Training* (Birth Guru/Birth Muse, 2008); *Essentials of Prehospital Maternity Care* (Prentice Hall, 2005); and *Hoofprints in the Sand: Wild Horses of the Atlantic Coast* (as Bonnie S. Urquhart; Eclipse, 2002), as well as articles in publications as dissimilar as *Equus* and the *American Journal of Nursing*. She is an artist and photographer and has illustrated all her own books.

By profession, she is a Certified Nurse-Midwife and Women's Health Nurse Practitioner who welcomes babies into the world at a freestanding birth center in Lancaster County, Pa. She obtained her MSN from the University of Pennsylvania after completing her BSN at Southern Vermont College, and she spent 10 years attending births in tertiary-care hospitals before returning to out-of-hospital practice. Prior to her career in obstetrics, she worked as an urban paramedic in Connecticut.

Horses have been her passion from infancy. For nearly two decades, she has spent countless hours researching and photographing the private lives of wild horses in both Western and Eastern habitats. She has been riding, training, teaching, and learning since her early teens, from rehabilitating hard-luck horses to wrangling trail rides in Vermont and Connecticut. In her vanishing spare time, she explores the hills and hollows of Lancaster County astride her horses Andante and Sonata.

More information and a collection of her photographs can be found at her Web site, www.BonnieGruenberg.com Additional information about the Atlantic Coast horse herds is on the Web at www.WildHorse Islands.com

If you liked this book, you may enjoy other titles by the author:

The Wild Horse Dilemma: Conflicts and Controversies of the Atlantic Coast Herds (Quagga Press, 2015)

The Hoofprints Guide Series (Quagga Press, 2015)
Assateague
Chincoteague
Ocracoke
Shackleford Banks
Cumberland Island

Forthcoming

Wild Horse Vacations: Your Guide to the Atlantic Wild Horse Trail with Local Attractions and Amenities (Quagga Press, 2015)
Wild Horses! A Kids' Guide to the East Coast Herds (Quagga Press, 2015)

Visit QuaggaPress.com for details.

Made in United States
Orlando, FL
26 March 2022

16154569R10085